The
Cuisine
of
Normandy

The
CUISINE
of
NORMANDY

French Regional Cooking
with
Princess Marie-Blanche de Broglie

BY
MARIE-BLANCHE DE BROGLIE
WITH
HARRIET ZUKAS

Foreword by Simone Beck

Boston
HOUGHTON MIFFLIN COMPANY
1984

My thanks go first to Carole F. Clements, because this book would
have taken much longer to write if she had not intimately cooperated
in its preparation. Her professional approach to cooking and her
numerous capabilities provided exactly the kind of help I needed to test
the recipes. I thank her for the friendly and efficient support
she gave me during several months.

I want also to thank my husband for his encouragement, for his
valuable criticisms, and for the part he took in the testing:
I mean the tasting.

Library of Congress Cataloging in Publication Data
De Broglie, Marie-Blanche.
The cuisine of Normandy.
Includes index.
1. Cookery, French. 2. Normandy (France)—Social life
and customs. I. Zukas, Harriet. II. Title.
TX719.D33   1984   641.5944′2   84-9020
ISBN 0-395-36552-X

Printed in the United States of America

v 10 9 8 7 6 5 4 3 2 1

Map and part title drawings by Jean Meyer

Foreword by Simone Beck

Chère Marie-Blanche,

It is with pleasure and emotion that I greet the publication of your book, *The Cuisine of Normandy*.

With pleasure, because we both believe that a knowledge of the culinary traditions of one's own country is one of the best ways to forge ties with people of other countries — a good way, in fact, to reach everyone who thinks that the preparation and artful presentation of good food are an expression of the joy of life.

And with emotion, because in our youth we were sheltered in the same French province, Haute Normandie. We are both of the Norman race and thus hard-working, opinionated, adventurous. These qualities, blended with the fantasy and originality of Latin civilization, have left us an important culinary inheritance.

Endowed with a temperate climate, opulent Normandy has always known how to sustain and adapt an original culinary tradition. Its resources are varied and abundant: fish and shellfish from the nearby Atlantic Ocean; cream, butter, and cheese from its rich farmlands; meats and poultry from its green prairies; and apples, peaches, and apricots from its orchards. All of these products have led the Normans to construct an apparently simple family-style cuisine, rich in nutritive elements and delicate flavors. There has been no need for the elaborate, complicated recipes so much in vogue these days.

I am pleased to note that you share with my dear friend and colleague Julia Child and myself certain views on the evolution of American cooking habits and the need to adapt French recipes to

American products and the American way of life. Your combination of authentic recipes from our beloved Normandy and the modern techniques perfected in your cooking school makes *The Cuisine of Normandy* a cookbook of great charm and practicality. It introduces an important new area of French regional cooking to the American kitchen.

Meilleures amitiés,
Simca Beck

Contents

SUMMER

Three Country Picnics / 5

I.

II.

III.

A Smart Lunch for Friends en Route to Deauville / 58

AUTUMN

Four Menus to Please Hunting Friends / 69

I.

II.

III.

A Dinner from La Bastide du Roy / 124

WINTER

Dîner au Robinet / 135

L'Anniversaire de Maman / 141

Two Menus for Entertaining in the Kitchen / 147

Four Favorite Winter Menus / 160

I.

SPRING

Lunch at the Shore / 186

Two Dinners from the Sea / 191

I.

II.

Easter at La Coquetterie / 204

FAVORITE RECIPES

Entrées / 272

Vegetables and Salads / 282

Desserts / 285

Index / 289

How It All Began

No one would ever have thought that I was destined to cook. In fact, when I was a child the kitchen was considered off limits, and under no circumstances were we allowed to enter there. But I had a marvelous father, the Marquis de Bagneux, whose hobby it was to prepare Sunday lunch. Only on that day were we allowed access to that sacred place, where we were then allowed to put our hands in the flour and do absolutely anything else we wanted. And there my father reigned supreme as a sort of high priest of cuisine, under the admiring eyes of his children.

My father's meals were celebrations of the best and finest products the countryside could provide. He was a man of generous nature who enjoyed life, and he shared his enthusiasm with his many friends, whom he treated in the best possible way. He was very fond of meat, which he roasted perfectly. But his specialty was really the sauces, from the simplest mayonnaise or vinaigrette to the more sophisticated types, and he had a special flair for *sauce Madère* and *sauce Périgueux*. And I must say I never ate better kidneys than the ones he prepared for us and served with a *sauce Madère* — a dish in which all the components reached a perfect equilibrium with one another.

His taste for innards also gave us delicious beef tongues with a *sauce piquante,* a dish that is extremely popular in Normandy and that is almost always served at the beginning of banquets, wedding lunches, and special occasions. He sometimes gratified us with tripes *à la mode de Caen,* which had been cooking for three days on a corner of the wood stove in a special crock and into which he poured a bottle of dry white wine once a day.

The results of our forays into the kitchen were both good and bad. By two o'clock in the afternoon we always had a wonderful lunch, but it took hours to clean up the kitchen after us. In spite of ourselves, though, we children learned several solid principles of cooking. The most important one that I learned was not only to use good products but to respect their quality. In my father's mind, products of superior quality should not be blended with inferior ones. For instance, he would not have used a cheap wine to make a sauce. And he used to say that the garnish of a course was there to enhance it and should never hide its genuine taste. That is why he was very careful when making sauces to avoid giving one component an excessive prominence, which could be detrimental to other ingredients.

My memories of those sessions left me with a real love of cooking. Cooking is a joy to me, and I owe that wholly to my father. My contemporary menus for entertaining are less extravagant than his, but I take just as much pleasure as he did in presenting them. We must cook in accordance with the way we live today, and foods chosen at the height of the season and prepared to retain their original flavors make the most perfect dishes I can imagine.

As time passed, Sunday lunches gave way to other, more grown-up pleasures. After several happy years as a student, far removed from any household worries, I married Prince François de Broglie, whose family has given France numerous generals, three field marshals, two prime ministers, and one winner of a Nobel Prize in physics. We did a lot of entertaining during our first years of marriage; friends, families, and business associates of my husband were often invited to our home.

One evening after a party I realized that I had been so preoccupied with activities in the kitchen that I had not been able to enjoy my guests. I was simply not well organized. My husband suggested cooking lessons, and I agreed. I chose the Cordon Bleu school, which is just down the street from our Paris apartment. At the beginning I was sure that six weeks of lessons would be ample — in fact, more than ample. In reality, however, those first six weeks only served to show up my ignorance. But I made up my mind to get my diploma, and so I worked on. A year and half later I was awarded the *grand diplôme* from the Cordon Bleu school.

It was a big step from taking courses to giving cooking lessons myself, though. I took that step by accident one day, at the request of several of my friends. They felt that the existing Paris cooking schools were geared toward beginners who wanted to become professionals. There was nowhere for housewives like themselves to go, nowhere for someone who simply wanted to learn better techniques and new dishes without devoting long periods of time to doing so. I began teaching a few friends at Monday evening *gastronomique* meetings, and in 1975 I finally decided to open my own school.

This book, then, is the result of the experience of a hostess who inadvertently became the owner of a cooking school. I must say in all honesty that I am not a chef, and I refuse to be considered one. A chef is someone who spends eight hours a day in the kitchen, working with, and assisted by, several people. I, on the other hand, am a modern princess, a woman who works, travels a great deal, manages a home, and raises children — all with very little help. Hence the name of my Paris school: Princesse Ère (era) 2001.

In this book I hope to prove that when one loves to do something and knows how to organize oneself, one can obtain excellent results and still be able to spend time with family and guests. That is why timing is so important. To master this problem fully, you must simply take into account several factors. First, you must know how much time it takes to make each recipe. Then you should take advantage of the fact that in numerous recipes, you can make several steps well in advance, sometimes the day or the morning before a dinner. We should also note that in various cases you can organize work so you can proceed with several steps simultaneously. And finally, many courses can be kept waiting quite a long time, provided you take appropriate care. For instance, you can maintain a hollandaise or béarnaise sauce for quite a while in a *bain-marie* if you add cold water from time to time before the sauce gets really warm. Or you can keep a soufflé waiting before cooking if you carefully fold the egg whites into the hot custard. Or you can cook a duck with turnips in the morning, cut it into pieces when it is cold (which is easier than cutting it when it's hot), and then place it on a platter covered with aluminum foil. Placed in an oven preset at its lowest temperature, the duck will hold until the evening, when you warm the sauce and turnips at the last minute.

Tricks of this kind help to solve two problems that face a hostess: how to greet and enjoy guests and yet serve elegant, delicious meals within specific time limitations. In all of my classes I insist that students have complete understanding of timing when they prepare a recipe. I want my students to feel relaxed when entertaining friends or family, and to enjoy the pleasures of cooking.

During the past five years I have been lucky enough to be invited regularly by American cooking schools to give classes in the United States. This experience has taught me a great deal, and I have found in the United States a wealth of excellent ideas. For instance, I love American salads, which look so gay, appetizing, and colorful. There exists in America a sense of color that extends not only to the courses for a meal but to plates and to kitchens. (I have seen in the United States many kitchens where it is a real pleasure to have a meal, whereas they remain the exception in France.) I have also rediscovered the barbecue, and hold a wonderful memory of some oysters that we bought on the shore in California, barbecued with melted butter and lemon juice, and ate accompanied with a cabernet from the Napa Valley.

It was during one of these trips that I met Harriet Zukas. Harriet lives in California and has organized culinary sessions for me there, and for the past three years I have had the pleasure of staying in the elegant and refined surroundings of her lovely house. Among Harriet's many qualities is her agreeable, easy-to-read style of writing. This book developed from our discussions about her excellent writing abilities and my desire to publish my recipes and convey my culinary style to readers as well. I warmly thank Harriet for her contribution to this book.

I hope in presenting this book to create a happy synthesis of American efficiency and the European sense of fantasy where food is concerned. I invite you to experience the changing seasons with me at my family's château, La Coquetterie, in Normandy. This is not cooking in the grand manner, as you might suspect — quite the contrary. It is in Normandy that my family is most informal and that I have the time to experiment in the kitchen. It is here that my cooking adventures began and that I hope you are going to feel at home. Welcome to La Coquetterie. *Bon appétit* and good cooking.

Marie-Blanche de Broglie

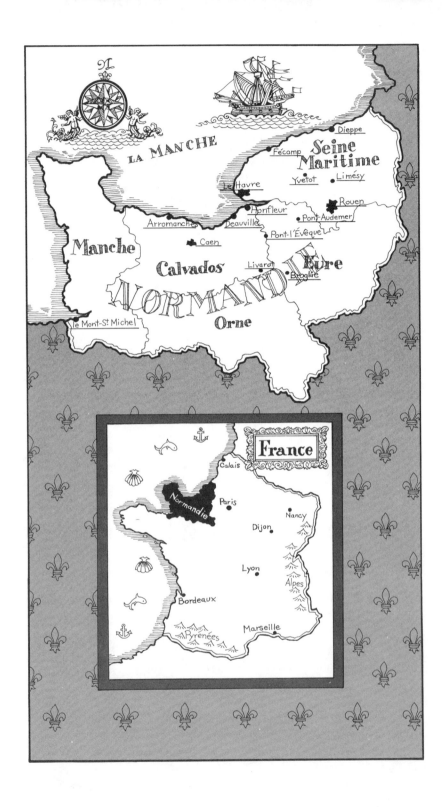

The Norman Table

Normandy is an area of about 10,000 square miles that is located about fifty miles west of Paris. It is a maritime province, offering almost 200 miles of shore on the English Channel and the Atlantic Ocean.

One of the richest parts of France and close to Paris, Normandy has always been important in the history of the country. It was invaded first by Romans en route to England, and then during the sixth or seventh century by the famous Vikings from the north. Some authorities state that *Norman* means "man of the north." This is quite possible, because the Vikings liked the countryside and settled in the region, where they married local women and became the Normans.

However, the Normans did not lose their taste for travel and adventure. During the eleventh century they invaded England with William the Conqueror; three centuries later they returned with the English king, who pretended to the French throne. But this time they were not welcome. Their attempt began the Hundred Years War, which ended some time after Joan of Arc was burned in Rouen in 1431. After that, Normandy's history was very peaceful until D-Day, June 6, 1944, when American and British troops landed on our shores and brought world attention to almost unknown places such as Arromanches, Sainte-Mère-l'Église, Omaha Beach, Utah Beach, and many others.

"My" area of Normandy is about one hundred miles from Paris, near Rouen, on the right bank of the Seine River. It is a region of green pasturelands, corn fields, and cattle. The wealth of the province is based on its cattle, which produce more than one-quarter of all the meat, milk, and dairy products of France. Our spotted white Normandy cows must have patches around their eyes, since the lack of these "spectacles" bars an animal from being entered in the herd book.

Velvety cream and salt-free butter contribute their richness to many Norman dishes, and our bakery shops are filled with buttery pastries, apple tarts, and brioche. In the little town of Broglie, where the head of my husband's family lives, there is a bakery, Les Trois Maréchaux, that makes the most beautiful brioche I have ever encountered.

Maître fromagers in Normandy tend their cheeses as if they were children and take great pride in presenting them in top form. Of the twenty-one different cheeses made in the region, Camembert, Pont-l'Évêque, and Livarot are certainly the celebrities. Marie Harel, a farmer's wife, is credited with inventing Camembert around 1790, and it is a superb example of soft, ripened cream cheese. Pont-l'Évêque is square and has a firm, elastic texture, although it falls in the category of soft cream cheeses. Livarot is stronger in flavor than Camembert or Pont-l'Évêque. Encircled by five bands of sedge, a grasslike herb, it is nicknamed *le colonel,* a reference to the five stripes on the sleeve of a French colonel's uniform.

You will find magnificent pear and apple orchards in Normandy, for fruit production is a very important industry. Pork and sausages from pigs raised in apple country have a special flavor, and Norman salt-marsh lamb is the best in France. In Rouen the oldest restaurant in France, La Couronne, still specializes in the famous duckling *à la Rouennaise.* (Speaking of ducks, I like to remember something my father used to say: "To eat a duck you need to be two: the duck and yourself.") Chicken dishes are typical Norman fare, as are omelettes of all kinds, from the simple ones of Mère Poulard at Mont-Saint-Michel to the more elaborate *Omelette à la Rouennaise,* with duck livers and red wine sauce, or *Omelette aux Pommes,* with apples and Calvados. Winged and four-footed game abounds in Normandy, forest mushrooms are plentiful, and watercress is cultivated in the running springs.

Normandy has still more to offer: an endless amount of seafood from its coastal waters — sole, shrimp, oysters, mussels, crab, lobsters, and scallops — as well as trout from the small rivers in our many valleys. A *Plateau de Fruits de Mer,* or shellfish platter, is a typical Norman first course.

Normandy produces no wine. Instead we make more than twenty different *crus* of cider, and the distillate of cider produces our great brandy, Calvados. Some ciders are sparkling and some are still; some are full-bodied and have a high alcohol content, while others are light and refreshingly spicy. When you are making a Norman dish that calls for hard cider and you cannot find any, use a dry white wine (to which you may add some apple brandy) rather than a sweet apple cider, since sweet cider tastes very little like hard cider and contains too much sugar.

Calvados takes its name from one of the districts in Normandy that is allowed to call its *eaux de vie* Calvados. The Pays d'Auge district, however, produces the best Calvados, and its apples are controlled just like the fruit in grape-growing Appellation Contrôlée areas. To become Appellation Contrôlée Calvados, the apples must be grown, crushed and pressed, made into cider, and distilled within the boundaries of the Pays d'Auge. Normans not only enjoy Calvados at the end of a meal, but they practice the old custom of the *trou normand,* serving Calvados in the middle of a large meal to aid digestion and clean the palate for the following courses.

For hundreds of years farmers and fishermen have shipped the best produce of Normany down the Seine to Paris, where today's interest in authentic flavors and fresh, seasonal foods has made Norman products more popular then ever.

To the memory of my father,
the Marquis de Bagneux,
a warm-hearted gourmet
for whom the sense of good cooking
and the sense of friendship
were inseparable

SUMMER

Three Country Picnics
Sunday Lunch à la Façon de mon Père
Two Country Lunches à ma Façon
Buffet Around the Pool
A Parisian-Style June Lunch
A Smart Lunch for Friends
en Route to Deauville

Summers at La Coquetterie bring everyone in my family back together again. Young and old, we all have a deep affection for this picturesque château of patterned brick and flintstone in a little corner of France that we have succeeded in holding onto since the time of William the Conqueror. It is a lush area where we are surrounded by wheat fields, apple trees, and the spotted Norman cows that produce some of the best milk and cream in the world. In 790 or thereabouts, Charlemagne ordered his subjects to plant the apple trees, realizing that damp, temperate regions are better for growing apples than grapes. His decision continues to influence the preparation of traditional Norman dishes, in which apples, cider, and Calvados play an important role. However, we prepare a great variety of dishes at the château, basing our choices on what we find at the Place du Vieux Marché in Rouen on market days, when it seems to overflow with produce from all over France.

The changeable climate of Normandy has taught us to be most flexible when planning our summer entertainments. A lunch begun in the garden often ends up in the house; on the other hand, whenever the sun decides to smile on us, we quickly move a party outdoors.

The Norman summer is the period of greatest abundance. Apples, pears, peaches, and apricots appear in the orchards, wild mushrooms and blackberries in the woods. At the time that our second crop of raspberries appears, in August, we begin the harvest of the wheat. Suddenly it is dry enough to have picnics, and friends of all ages start to arrive.

My first childhood memories of summer picnics are of impromptu affairs arranged in haste during the Second World War by my mother and father as quick escapes from the house and into the fields. For the children's sake my parents tried to treat the war as a kind of game. We often sat with our picnic and watched the rockets fly over our house like drunken birds — the Germans had taken over my grandmother's château, twelve kilometers away, and were firing the rockets across the Channel into England. Sometimes one of them would land on our property, and my father referred to those as the latest gifts from his mother-in-law.

During the war the food was extremely simple. A cold chicken, a salad, and fruit made a nice menu then, and was enough to help us forget, at least during an afternoon, the difficulties of the time. My taste for picnics comes from those days.

THREE COUNTRY PICNICS

I

Pâté de Canard au Calvados
Duck Pâté with Calvados and Prunes

Gâteau Piperade
Three-Layered Omelette with Peppers

Salade d'Épinards Crus aux Agrumes
Spinach Salad with Honey and Oranges

Mirlitons de Rouen
Almond Tartlets

Wine: A red wine from Côtes de Provence with
the whole menu

This is a gay menu as full of color as the marketplace in Rouen in the summertime, when it is brightened considerably with an alluring array of glorious tomatoes and red and yellow peppers from the south. The salad reflects my fondness for oranges. For me, oranges wrapped in silver paper were one of the nicest parts of Christmas, and they still remain, for me, the symbol of a feast.

Pâté de Canard au Calvados

Duck Pâté with Calvados and Prunes

Serves 6

The famous Rouen duckling is a combination of domestic duck and wild duck from the Seine estuary. Domestic duck works very well in this typically Norman pâté, which should be made a day or two in advance.

> **A 4½ to 5 pound duck, boned, or**
>   **2 large duck breasts and 2 dark chicken**
>   **quarters, including thighs and drumsticks**
> **½ cup Calvados**
> **½ onion**
> **2 shallots**
> **1 apple, peeled and cored**
> **1 tablespoon butter**
> **10 ounces loose sausage (mild "country" brands are**
>   **best)**
> **1 egg**
> **Salt and freshly ground pepper**
> **Allspice or four-spice mixture, to taste**
> **Thyme, to taste**
> **1 tablespoon minced fresh sage or scant**
>   **½ teaspoon dried sage**
> **6 prunes, pitted and quartered**
> **1 small bay leaf**
> **2 whole sage leaves**
> **2 strips bacon or skin from chicken**

Remove all the meat from the bones of the duck and chicken. Cut one duck breast into ¼-inch strips and the rest of the meat into chunks. Marinate the meat in the Calvados for at least one hour.

Mince the onion, shallots, and apple; sauté them gently in butter. Using a grinder or food processor, chop the chunks of meat coarsely. Combine this meat, the sausage, and the onion-apple mixture. Moisten it with the egg, add the seasonings and the Calvados, and mix well. Fry or bake a small patty and check the seasoning.

Place one-third of the mixture in the bottom of an oiled 3½-cup loaf pan or terrine. Then place half of the breast strips and the prunes on top, lengthwise; cover with another third of the meat mixture, and repeat. Put the bay leaf and sage leaves on top and cover with the bacon or chicken skin and foil.

Bake the pâté in a water bath in a preheated 325°F oven until done, about 1½ hours. Weight the pan until the pâté is cool (another pan with a can of tomatoes on top works well). Refrigerate it for a day or two before serving.

Gâteau Piperade

Three-Layered Omelette with Peppers

Serves 6

For the tomato sauce:
2 shallots, minced
2 tablespoons butter
6 medium tomatoes, peeled, seeded, and chopped
1 clove garlic, crushed
* Bouquet garni made with basil sprigs and extra
     thyme
Salt and freshly ground pepper
Pinch of sugar (optional)

For the omelette:
1 small green pepper, seeded and thinly sliced
1 small red pepper, seeded and thinly sliced
2 tablespoons vegetable oil
1 cup sliced scallions
12 eggs
Salt and freshly ground pepper
Tabasco sauce
2 to 3 tablespoons chopped fresh basil or thyme
3 tablespoons butter
6 tablespoons grated Parmesan cheese
Small black niçoise olives (for garnish)

To make the tomato sauce:
Sauté the shallots in the butter until they are transparent. Add the tomatoes, garlic, and bouquet garni and cook until the liquid has evaporated, stirring occasionally. Add salt and pepper to taste and a pinch of sugar if the sauce is too acid. You may make the sauce in advance and reheat it before assembling the *gâteau*.

To make the omelette:
Sauté the green and red peppers separately in 1 tablespoon of oil until they are just tender. Remove and drain them. Sauté the scallions gently in the second tablespoon of oil until they are wilted and transparent, strain them, and reserve.

Break 3 eggs into a bowl and beat them with salt, pepper, 2 or 3 drops of Tabasco sauce, and a quarter of the chopped fresh herbs. Heat 1 tablespoon of butter over medium heat in a small skillet until foamy. Add the egg mixture and cook until it is set. Sprinkle it with half the green pepper and 2 tablespoons of the grated Parmesan cheese. Continue cooking 1 minute, then finish it under the broiler to set the top and melt the cheese. Place this omelette on a warm serving platter and spread it with tomato sauce.

Repeat this procedure three times, using the scallions and red pepper instead of the green pepper and cheese for every other omelette. Place each omelette on top of the previous one. Spread them all with tomato sauce except for the top one; sprinkle it with the remaining herbs and garnish it with olives. You may pass the remaining tomato sauce at the table.

Salade d'Épinards Crus aux Agrumes

Spinach Salad with Honey and Oranges

Serves 8

1 pound fresh spinach, washed and with stems
    removed
½ small head red cabbage
½ large celery root, peeled and cut into matchsticks
3 tablespoons lemon juice or vinegar
3 oranges
1 grapefruit
4 scallions, sliced
1 avocado, sliced

For the dressing:
3 tablespoons honey
4 to 5 tablespoons juice from the citrus fruits
½ teaspoon paprika
Salt and freshly ground pepper
⅓ cup oil
2 tablespoons minced parsley

Wash the spinach well and blot it dry on paper towels. Shred the cabbage finely. Cook the celery root in boiling salted water with lemon juice or vinegar for 3 to 5 minutes, drain, and refresh it under cold water. Peel and section the oranges and grapefruit.

Combine the spinach, cabbage, and celery root in a salad bowl. Top with the orange and grapefruit sections and the scallions. Add the avocado slices just before serving.

Combine all the ingredients for the salad dressing in a cruet or jar. Taste, and correct seasoning if necessary. Toss the salad with the dressing and serve it on chilled plates.

Mirlitons de Rouen

Almond Tartlets

Makes 8 to 10 small tarts (3 to 3½ inches)

Many types of almond tartlets are made in Normandy. The *mirlitons* made in Rouen are my favorite, and are perfect for picnics.

* About ¾ pound puff pastry scraps or demi-puff
    pastry
1 jar apricot jam
2 eggs
⅓ cup sugar
⅓ cup ground almonds
Almond extract, to taste
Slivered almonds (for topping)

Roll out the pastry thinly and line several 3- to 4-inch tart molds with it. Chill the shells well and then brush them with melted apricot jam. Beat the eggs and sugar until they are thick and light in color. Add the ground almonds and a few drops of almond extract; mix. Fill the molds about three-fourths full with the egg mixture. Sprinkle each tartlet lightly with slivered almonds, then bake them in a preheated 375°F oven until they are puffed and browned, about 15 to 20 minutes.

THREE COUNTRY PICNICS

II

Soupe Glacée aux Poivrons Rouges
Iced Red Pepper Soup

Clafoutis de Courgettes
Zucchini Flan

Pâté de Veau et de Poulet au Fenouil
Terrine of Veal and Chicken with Fennel

Coeur à la Crème aux Fraises
Coeur à la Crème with Strawberries

Wine: A Fleurie with the whole menu

Picnics should be as carefree as possible, and for this menu you make everything in advance. I like to choose vibrant colors and interesting textures for summer meals to be served out-of-doors. These dishes will delight the eye even in a garden filled with brilliant flowers.

Soupe Glacée aux Poivrons Rouge

Iced Red Pepper Soup

Serves 6

4 leeks, chopped (white part only)
4 red peppers, seeded and chopped
3 tablespoons butter
* 4 cups chicken stock, well degreased
¼ teaspoon thyme
½ teaspoon crumbled bay leaf
* 1 cup *crème fraîche* or sour cream
Salt and freshly ground white pepper
1 red pepper, cut in julienne strips (for garnish)

In a large, heavy saucepan, sauté the leeks and peppers in the butter over low heat, covered, for 15 minutes, or until the vegetables are soft. Add one cup of the chicken stock and the thyme and bay leaf, bring the mixture to a boil, turn down the heat, and simmer, covered, for 30 minutes.

Purée the cooked mixture in a blender or food processor. Pour it into a large bowl and add the remaining stock and the *crème fraîche* or sour cream. Season to taste with salt and pepper and chill the soup, covered, for several hours. Serve it garnished with julienne strips of red pepper.

Clafoutis de Courgettes

Zucchini Flan

Serves 6

Although I serve this at room temperature for lunch, it is equally good hot, as a first course or as an accompaniment to roast meat.

> 2 pounds (6 to 8) small zucchini, scrubbed and
>   trimmed
> 1 tablespoon coarse salt
> 2 tablespoons butter
> 4 eggs
> 3 ounces cream cheese, softened
> 2 ounces (about ½ cup) grated Swiss cheese
> 2 ounces grated Parmesan cheese
> 1 tablespoon minced fresh tarragon or ½ teaspoon
>   dried tarragon
> 1 tablespoon minced fresh chives or scallion tops
> Pinch of thyme
> Salt and freshly ground pepper
> Nutmeg, freshly ground

Cut the zucchini into thin slices. (This can be done in a food processor.) Place them in a colander, sprinkle with salt, toss gently, and set aside to drain for ½ hour. Rinse, drain, and press them dry on paper towels.

Melt the butter in a large skillet. Add the zucchini and sauté them quickly over fairly high heat for about 5 minutes, shaking the pan occasionally to prevent sticking.

Beat the eggs very well with the softened cream cheese in a bowl. Add the Swiss cheese and about half the Parmesan cheese, reserving the rest for the top. Add the herbs and season to taste with salt, pepper, and nutmeg.

Mix the eggs with the zucchini and place them in a well-buttered 8-inch round or square baking dish. Top with the remaining Parmesan and bake in the center of a preheated 350°F oven until the flan is set and browned, about 20 minutes. Serve warm or tepid.

Pâté de Veau et de Poulet au Fenouil

Terrine of Veal and Chicken with Fennel

Serves 8

This should be made at least a day in advance.

- 1 large whole chicken breast, boned
- 1 pound boneless veal
- 1 pound boneless pork
- ½ cup Cognac
- ½ teaspoon fennel seed
- Pinch of dried thyme
- ½ teaspoon dried tarragon
- Salt and freshly ground pepper
- 1 clove garlic, minced
- ¼ pound salt pork, cut in 1-inch cubes and blanched
- 1 medium onion, finely chopped
- 1 small bulb fennel, finely chopped
- 3 tablespoons butter
- 1 tablespoon minced fresh tarragon
- 2 eggs, beaten
- Allspice, to taste
- ⅓ cup pistachios
- 1 bay leaf

Slice half the chicken breast and a third of the veal into strips. Cut the rest of the meat into chunks, and marinate both the chunks and the strips in a glass bowl with the Cognac, fennel seed, thyme, tarragon, salt, pepper, and garlic, at least 4 hours (or overnight).

Remove the strips of chicken and veal, then pour off and reserve the marinade. Combine half the chunks of meat with half the cubed, blanched salt pork and chop coarsely in a food processor, or mince by hand. Remove this meat and chop the remaining meat and salt pork. Combine the chopped meat in a mixing bowl.

Sauté the onion and fennel gently in the butter until they are wilted. Mix with the meat and add the fresh tarragon, reserved marinade, eggs, and allspice, salt, and freshly ground pepper to taste; mix well to combine. Make a small patty and fry or bake it; taste, and correct the seasoning. The flavor should be spicy.

Oil a 6-cup loaf pan or terrine and fill it one-third full with the chopped-meat mixture. Arrange half the strips of veal and chicken on top, sprinkle them with half the pistachios, and cover with half the remaining meat mixture, pressing it down gently. Repeat with the remaining strips and nuts, covering them with a layer of chopped meat. Place the bay leaf on top and cover the terrine with buttered foil and a lid, if possible.

Place the terrine in a baking pan and add boiling water until it comes halfway up the sides of the terrine. Bake in a preheated 350°F oven about 1½ hours, until the pâté has pulled away from the sides of the terrine and the juices are clear. Remove the terrine and place a weight on top until the meat is cool; then keep it in the refrigerator.

To serve, unmold or slice the pâté in the terrine and serve it with pickles and mustard, if desired.

Coeur à la Crème aux Fraises

Coeur à la Crème with Strawberries

Serves 8

2 cups cottage cheese
1¼ cups (10 ounces) cream cheese
¼ cup confectioner's sugar
1 cup very heavy cream or *crème fraîche*
Fresh strawberries (for garnish)

Force the cottage cheese through a sieve, or blend it in a food processor until smooth. Beat in the softened cream cheese, sugar, and heavy cream or *crème fraîche*. (For a lighter texture, whip the cream first and fold it into the sweetened cheese mixture.)

Line a heart-shaped mold that has draining holes with cheese-cloth, and pack the mixture firmly into it. Cover the mold with a plate, weight it, and refrigerate it overnight. To serve, turn out the molded dessert onto a plate and surround it with fresh strawberries.

THREE COUNTRY PICNICS

III: CHRISTIANE'S PICNIC

Ratatouille en Gelée
Ratatouille in Aspic

Rôti de Veau Piqué au Jambon
Cold Roast Veal Studded with Ham

Oeufs Durs Farcis aux Anchois
Deviled Eggs with Anchovies

Tarte aux Reine-Claudes
Greengage Plum Tart

Wine: A Rosé de Provence with the whole menu

As I said before, no war took place in Normandy during the five centuries between the death of Joan of Arc and World War II, which explains why this area is still full of châteaux of all styles and sizes. My cousin Christiane owns one of them, an eighteenth-century château in a region known as the Perche, a district famous for stock breeding and for the powerful draft horses known as Percherons.

A drive to Christiane's is always a delightful summer diversion. The wooded hills and deep green valleys of the Perche offer a lovely change from the flat farmlands of our plateau. Christiane comes to Normandy to ride her horses, so she plans festive but casual parties for which everything can be prepared in advance. A sportswoman who likes healthful food and fresh products, Christiane grows her own vegetables and raises her own chickens to insure that she obtains the freshest eggs.

Ratatouille en Gelée

Ratatouille in Aspic

Serves 6 to 8

For the ratatouille:
2 red bell peppers
3 large onions
2 eggplants
3 zucchini
4 tomatoes
2 cloves garlic
6 to 7 tablespoons olive oil
2 sprigs fresh thyme or ½ teaspoon dried thyme
Salt and freshly ground pepper

For the aspic:
2 envelopes gelatin
* ⅓ cup cold stock or water
  1½ cups cooking liquid from ratatouille,
    degreased, or stock, or consommé
Salt and freshly ground pepper
Tabasco sauce, to taste
1 tablespoon lemon juice or vinegar
2 to 3 tablespoons Madeira

For the sauce:
* 1 cup *crème fraîche* or whipped heavy cream
  ¼ teaspoon grated raw garlic or garlic juice
  1 teaspoon chopped chives (optional)

To make the ratatouille (it is easiest to prepare this the day before):
Wash and dry the peppers, remove their seeds, and cut them into
strips. Peel and slice the onions. Wash and dry the eggplants,
zucchini, and tomatoes. Peel and cube the eggplants, slice the

zucchini, and peel, seed, and quarter the tomatoes. Peel and mince the garlic.

Heat the oil in a large, heavy casserole with a lid. Add the peppers, onion, and eggplants and brown them; then add the zucchini and cook for 10 minutes, stirring from time to time. Add the tomatoes, garlic, and thyme, stirring to blend, and salt and pepper to taste. Cook for 20 minutes, then remove the ratatouille from the heat and drain it in a colander for about 2 hours, reserving the juices for the aspic.

To make the aspic:
Soften the gelatin in the stock or water, then dissolve it. Add it to the degreased ratatouille cooking liquid, stock, or consommé (the aspic will jell more quickly if this is cold). Canned consommé is satisfactory, especially if you combine it with cooking liquid, but if you use jelled consommé, reduce the additional gelatin to only 1 tablespoon. Season the aspic rather highly with salt and pepper, Tabasco sauce, lemon juice or vinegar, and Madeira.

To mold the ratatouille:
Pour a layer of aspic about ⅜-inch thick into the bottom of a 10-inch loaf pan and chill to set. Remove 8 to 10 strips of pepper and an equal number of zucchini rounds from the ratatouille, dry them on a paper towel, and arrange them in the mold; cover them with more aspic and chill to set. Then add a layer of ratatouille to half-fill the mold, and another layer of aspic. Allow this to set before filling the mold with the rest of the vegetable mixture and aspic. Chill it 4 hours or overnight.

To make the sauce:
Place the *crème fraîche* or whipped cream in a bowl and add the garlic or garlic juice and chives, stirring to mix them thoroughly.

To serve, unmold the aspic onto a serving platter and top it with a dollop of sauce. Pass the remaining sauce in a sauceboat.

Rôti de Veau Piqué au Jambon

Cold Roast Veal Studded with Ham

Serves 8

3 pounds boneless veal roast (top round, sirloin,
    or sirloin tip), tied in a cylinder
4 or 5 long strips of ham and bacon
Pistachio nuts (optional)
1 to 2 tablespoons oil
1 carrot, sliced
1 onion, sliced
* Bouquet garni

With a larding needle, insert the strips of ham and bacon
lengthwise into the roast. Alternate them with pistachios placed in
the ends for color, if you like.

Brown the roast in the oil in a heavy Dutch oven, turning it
frequently. Add the vegetables after 5 minutes. When the meat is
browned, add the bouquet garni, cover the casserole, and place it
in a preheated 325°F oven for about 1¼ hours, or until a meat
thermometer inserted in the veal reaches 170°F. Baste the meat
several times during cooking. When it is done, remove it from the
oven, cool it thoroughly, and refrigerate. Slice and serve cold or at
room temperature.

Oeufs Durs Farcis aux Anchois

Deviled Eggs with Anchovies

Serves 8

> 8 eggs
> Vinegar
> 1 teaspoon capers
> 3 or 4 anchovy fillets
> * 2 tablespoons mayonnaise
> 1 tablespoon cream
> 1 teaspoon Dijon mustard
> Freshly ground pepper
> 2 teaspoons minced fresh chives
> Lemon juice (optional)
> Minced parsley (for garnish)
> Bits of truffle (for garnish)

Boil the eggs for 9 or 10 minutes in water containing several tablespoons of vinegar. Refresh them in cold water, crack the shells in several places, and cool in cold water.

Peel and halve the eggs and carefully remove their yolks. Mash the yolks, capers, and anchovy fillets by hand or in a food processor, then moisten them with the mayonnaise and cream, adding more if necessary. Season to taste with mustard, pepper, minced chives, and a few drops of lemon juice if desired.

Pipe or spoon the yolk mixture into the egg whites. Arrange them on a platter and decorate them with minced parsley and bits of truffle.

Tarte aux Reine-Claudes

Greengage Plum Tart

Serves 6

This tart may be made with any type of plum or with apricots, cherries, or grapes. If you use grapes, you do not need to cook them.

* 1 recipe *pâte sucrée*
  3 tablespoons apricot jam, warmed
  1 cup water
  1 cup sugar
  Juice of ½ lemon
  2 pounds greengage plums
  8 ounces cream cheese (at room temperature)
  ½ cup whipping cream
  ½ cup sugar
  2 large eggs
  Grated zest of 1 lemon
  ½ teaspoon vanilla extract
  4 tablespoons apricot jam, heated and strained
      (for glaze)

Roll out the *pâte sucrée* about ⅛-inch thick and line a 9- or 10-inch tart pan with it. Trim the edges. Chill the shell for 30 minutes, then line it with aluminum foil, fill it with dried beans or rice, and bake it in the lower third of a preheated 400°F oven for 15 minutes. Remove the foil and dried beans. Paint the shell with the 3 tablespoons of warmed apricot jam and return it to the oven for 10 minutes more, until it is a light gold.

To poach the fruit, combine the water, 1 cup of sugar, and the lemon juice in a saucepan and simmer about 5 minutes to dissolve the sugar. Halve the plums, remove their pits, and add them to the simmering liquid. Poach them until just tender, about 5 or 6 minutes. Remove them with a slotted spoon, drain them on paper towels, and cool.

To make the filling, place the cream cheese, cream, ½ cup of sugar, eggs, lemon zest, and vanilla in a food processor or blender and blend them until smooth. Pour the filling into the shell and bake the tart in the middle of a preheated 350°F oven for 30 minutes. Remove it from the oven and cool it on a rack.

Arrange the plums cut side down and close together on the tart, and brush them with the 4 tablespoons of apricot jam. Chill the tart for 1 hour before serving.

SUNDAY LUNCH
À LA FAÇON DE MON PÈRE

IV

Homards à la Nage
Baby Lobsters Swimming in Court Bouillon

Carré d'Agneau à l'Estragon
Rack of Lamb with Tarragon

Fonds d'Artichaut Farcis Strasbourg
Artichoke Bottoms with Foie Gras and
Mushrooms

Salade de Laitue aux Oeufs de Caille
Green Salad with Quail Eggs

Plateau de Fromages Normands
Tray of Norman Cheeses
(Camembert, Pont-l'Évêque, Neufchâtel)

Gâteau Meringué aux Noisettes
Hazelnut Meringue Cake

Wine: Champagne with the whole menu

My father loved to entertain and did so continually. Because he was on the board of a champagne company, he often served champagne or nonsparkling wines from the Champagne area. Red wines from the villages of Bouzy and Sillery, which produce the best red grapes of Champagne, were favorites, as was the Avize Blanc de Blancs, a very light champagne made with grapes from Avize, another village that is famous for the quality of its vineyards. These wines he found to be not only extremely good but light and refreshing in the summer months. And they were generally a surprise for his guests, because they are not normally available for sale.

My father took great pains in selecting the food he cooked for Sunday lunch and thought nothing of driving to the coast to buy baby lobsters from the fishermen who pitched their stands near the beach. He never tired of the delicate lamb raised on the salty meadows near Mont-Saint-Michel, and he considered Norman cheeses to be the best in the world. No meal was complete without several cheeses from which to choose. My father loved desserts but had no interest in attempting to make them, so they were always prepared in advance by others.

Homards à la Nage

Baby Lobsters Swimming in Court Bouillon

Serves 6

This is a favorite way of preparing the small lobsters known in Normandy as *demoiselles* of Cherbourg.

For the court bouillon:
1 bottle dry white wine
3 cups water
2 carrots, sliced
2 onions, sliced
4 shallots, sliced
10 peppercorns
5 sprigs parsley
1 sprig fresh thyme or ½ teaspoon dried thyme
1 sprig fresh tarragon
1 bay leaf
1 leek (green part only)

6 small live lobsters (about 1 pound each)
3 tablespoons Calvados
1 tablespoon minced fresh parsley
6 ounces butter, cut in small pieces
Parsley sprigs (for garnish)

To make the court bouillon, put the wine, water, vegetables, and peppercorns into a large pot with a cover. Make a bouquet garni by wrapping the herbs in the leek greens and tying them together with string. Add this to the pot, bring the mixture to a boil, and simmer, uncovered, for 15 minutes.

To prepare the lobsters, return the court bouillon to a boil, plunge the lobsters into it, cover, and simmer for 8 to 10 minutes. Remove the lobsters, reserving the liquid.

Using a strong, sharp-pointed knife, split the bodies lengthwise. Discard the dark intestinal vein, the sac at the head, and the spongy gray lungs, and crack the claws. Pour a ladleful of the court bouillon over the lobsters and keep them warm.

Remove the bouquet garni from the court bouillon, strain the liquid, and reduce it by about one-half over high heat. Add the Calvados and correct the seasoning if necessary. Add the minced parsley, and whisk in the butter.

Place the lobsters on a serving dish, garnish them with parsley sprigs, and serve the sauce in individual small bowls.

Carré d'Agneau à l'Estragon

Rack of Lamb with Tarragon

Serves 6 to 8

This is my version of the classic *carré d'agneau persillé*. Fresh tarragon is sold in large bouquets in France. If the amount called for in the recipe proves difficult to obtain, you may use half tarragon and half parsley.

> 2 racks or ribs lamb, 4 pounds each untrimmed,
>   or 2 pounds each trimmed
> Salt and freshly ground pepper
> Garlic (optional)
> ½ cup minced fresh tarragon
> 1 cup fresh white bread crumbs
> 2 to 3 tablespoons butter, melted
> * 1 cup brown stock, or ⅓ cup white wine and
>   ⅔ cup water
> Watercress (for garnish)

Season the lamb with salt and pepper. Rub it with garlic, if you wish. Place it in a preheated 400°F oven and roast it for about 20 minutes.

Meanwhile, mix together the tarragon and bread crumbs and moisten them with the melted butter. Remove the lamb from the oven and cover it with the bread-crumb mixture, spooning on any pan drippings.

Continue roasting the lamb to the desired doneness, about 20 minutes more for medium rare (160°F on a meat thermometer). Let stand 10 to 15 minutes before carving.

Deglaze the roasting pan with the stock or wine and water, scraping the bottom of the pan well. Degrease and reduce the gravy, if desired, to intensify its flavor.

To serve, slice the roast into chops, then reassemble the racks on a warm platter. Garnish them with watercress and place cutlet frills on the ends of the bones if you wish. Pass the gravy in a sauceboat.

Fonds d'Artichaut Farcis Strasbourg

Stuffed Artichoke Bottoms with Foie Gras and Mushrooms

Serves 6

6 large artichokes or 6 frozen artichoke bottoms
Lemon juice
Salt

For the duxelles:
2 ounces mushrooms
1 tablespoon minced scallions
2 tablespoons butter
1 tablespoon chopped fresh parsley
Salt and freshly ground pepper

6 tablespoons *pâté de foie gras*
2 tablespoons butter, melted
Freshly ground pepper
¼ cup Madeira and/or water

Break off the stems of the artichokes next to the base. Holding a sharp paring knife parallel to the vegetable, remove the leaves, turning the artichoke against the knife blade. Cut off the top above the fuzzy parts. Rub the artichokes with lemon juice to prevent discoloration. Cook, covered, in boiling salted water with the juice of half a lemon until tender, 30 to 40 minutes. Drain and refresh them in cold water. (If you are using frozen artichokes, cook them according to the directions on the package, then drain and refresh them.)

To make the *duxelles*, clean the mushrooms and cut off their stems. Roughly chop them with the scallions. Melt the butter in a large skillet, add the mushrooms and scallions, and sauté them for 10 minutes. Purée them in a food processor, add the parsley, and season with salt and pepper.

Scoop out each choke with a teaspoon and line the artichokes with *duxelles*. Put the *foie gras* in the centers and drizzle with butter. Sprinkle the artichokes with pepper and Madeira or water. Bake them in a preheated oven for 15 minutes at 400°F or for 20 minutes at 375°F.

Salade de Laitue aux Oeufs de Caille

Green Salad with Quail Eggs

Serves 6

If quail eggs are unavailable, you may substitute three hard-boiled chicken eggs. Sieve the yolks and whites separately and sprinkle them over the salad.

2 heads Bibb lettuce
12 quail eggs
2 tablespoons vinegar
1 teaspoon finely minced parsley, tarragon, or chives

For the vinaigrette:
1 teaspoon Dijon mustard
1 tablespoon lemon juice
2 teaspoons vinegar
6 to 7 tablespoons oil
Salt and freshly ground pepper

Wash the lettuce well, spin dry, and wrap it in towels. Keep it in a plastic bag in the refrigerator until you are ready to use it.

Bring the quail eggs to a boil in water to which you have added vinegar and simmer until they are hard-cooked, 8 to 10 minutes. Cool them in cold running water, and peel.

Place all of the ingredients for the vinaigrette in a small jar with a lid and shake to combine them. Pour the dressing into a small sauceboat.

Arrange the largest lettuce leaves around the bottom of a salad bowl, then arrange the next largest leaves, graduating to the smallest leaves. You will have formed what looks like a large head of lettuce. Tuck the quail eggs among the leaves and sprinkle with the herbs. Toss the salad with the vinaigrette at the table.

Gâteau Meringué aux Noisettes

Hazelnut Meringue Cake

Serves 8 to 10

Do not let the number of steps in this recipe discourage you. Thanks to electric mixers and food processors, you can accomplish all of them without difficulty, and the result is a luxurious cake well worth your time.

For the hazelnut cake:
3 large eggs
½ cup cake flour or ⅓ cup all-purpose flour plus 2
    tablespoons cornstarch
½ teaspoon baking powder
1¼ cups (4 ounces) ground hazelnuts, made from
    ¾ cup whole hazelnuts
¾ cup sugar
2 teaspoons vanilla extract
4 ounces (1 stick) butter, melted

For the meringue:
4 egg whites
¼ teaspoon cream of tartar or salt
1 cup sugar
1⅓ cups (4½ ounces) ground hazelnuts, made from
    1 cup whole hazelnuts
1 tablespoon cornstarch
1 tablespoon vanilla extract

For the chocolate cream:
1 cup heavy cream
8 ounces bittersweet chocolate, cut in small pieces
1 tablespoon rum (optional)

To prepare the hazelnuts:
Toast all the nuts in a hot oven until their skins brown and start to crack. Remove the skins by rubbing the nuts vigorously against one another a handful at a time, either enclosed in a dish towel or between two strainers set one inside the other, then grind the nuts in a food processor. You will need a total of 8½ ounces of hazelnuts for this recipe. You may grind the amount for the cake with the dry ingredients, but for the meringue, grind the nuts with 1 tablespoon of the sugar.

To make the cake:
Warm the eggs in a bowl of hot tap water; change the water if it becomes cold. Liberally butter and flour an 8- or 9-inch cake pan and line it with wax paper or parchment. Mix the flour, baking

powder, and hazelnuts in a bowl. Using a food processor or an electric mixer, beat the eggs with the sugar about 1 minute, until fluffy. Add the vanilla and melted butter and mix well, then add the dry ingredients and mix just to combine. Pour the batter into the prepared cake pan. Bake in a preheated 300°F oven until done, about 35 to 40 minutes. Cool the cake for 10 minutes in the pan, then unmold it and finish cooling on a wire rack. If you make it ahead of time, cool it, wrap it well, and freeze it.

To make the meringue layers:
Grease and flour a large baking sheet and mark two 8- or 9-inch circles — the same size as your cake pan — with a flan ring or pot lid; set aside. Beat the egg whites with the cream of tartar or salt until they form peaks, then add 2 tablespoons of sugar and continue beating until they are slightly glossy. Gently fold in the remaining sugar and the hazelnuts and cornstarch, adding them a third at a time. Fold in the vanilla. Fill a pastry bag fitted with a medium-sized plain tip with the meringue, and pipe a spiral to fill each of the premarked circles on the baking sheet. Pipe extra meringue into puffs for decoration. Bake in a preheated 275°F oven for 1 hour. Cooled meringues will keep for two weeks in an airtight container.

To make the chocolate cream:
Bring the cream to a boil, remove it from the heat, and add the chocolate. Stir until the chocolate has completely melted, then pour it into a mixing bowl and chill, stirring occasionally, until it is thick but not hard, about 30 minutes. Beat it with an electric mixer until it is light and fluffy and will hold soft peaks. Beat in the rum if you wish.

To assemble the cake:
Slice the cake into two layers. If the meringue layers are not the same size as the cake, trim them with a serrated knife. Cut a circle of cardboard the size of the cake to aid in handling, and put a dot of chocolate cream in its center. Place a meringue layer on top of it; spread the meringue with a thin layer of chocolate cream, and

top with a cake layer. Spread the cake with another thin layer of chocolate cream and place the other layer of cake on top. Spread this layer with chocolate cream and top with the second meringue. Spread the remaining chocolate cream around the sides of the cake; if you have any crusts of meringue or extra meringues, crush them and press them into the chocolate to finish the sides. Decorate the top with meringue puffs.

The assembled cake will benefit from standing at least 4 hours or as much as a day in the refrigerator, to blend flavors and soften the meringue. Leave the cake at room temperature for ½ hour before serving.

TWO COUNTRY LUNCHES
À MA FAÇON

I

Pamplemousse Césarée
Grapefruit Baskets with Cold Fish Salad

Colin aux Cèpes
Hake with Wild Mushrooms

Rendez-Vous des Primeurs
Mixed Baby Vegetables

Fromage
Cheese
(Camembert)

Fraises Cardinal
Strawberries in Raspberry Sauce

Wine: A Muscadet with the grapefruit and fish,
then a Saint-Amour

In this menu I use tarragon in both the fish and the vegetables. I believe in a continuity of flavors. Sharp contrasts in the fragrance of herbs lessen the character of the dishes they are expected to enhance.

The *Rendez-Vous des Primeurs* makes me think of the marvelous vegetable garden we had during the summer when I was a child. We grew everything we ate — asparagus, tomatoes, green beans, potatoes, and tiny peas (we children were obliged to shell them as punishment). The turnips and leeks we grew were seldom presented in the dining room but instead were reserved for stocks and sauces, since to the French mind they were not nourishing enough to be served on their own. You would be surprised at how recently French people began to enjoy such vegetables.

Pamplemousse Césarée

Grapefruit Baskets with Cold Fish Salad

Serves 6

>   1 pound firm white fish fillets (sole, flounder,
>   whitefish, etc.)
> * 1 quart fish stock, or water and clam juice
>   ½ pound carrots, peeled and sliced
>   ½ pound celery root, diced, or 6 to 8 celery stalks,
>   thinly sliced
>   5 medium grapefruit
>   2 apples
> * 1 cup mayonnaise
>   3 tablespoons tomato ketchup
>   Juice of ½ lemon, or to taste
>   3 tablespoons cream or sour cream
>   1 cup hazelnuts or pecans, chopped
>   Salt and freshly ground pepper
>   1 tablespoon chopped fresh mint (for garnish)
>   6 maraschino cherry halves (optional)

Poach the fish fillets in simmering fish stock or water to which you have added 3 cups of clam juice, until just cooked. Remove, drain, and cool. In the same liquid, cook the carrots and celery root. (If you are using stalks of celery, do not cook them.) When they are soft, remove and refresh in cold water. Cut three grapefruits in half and scoop out the meat, reserving the skins. Peel and section the remaining two, removing the seeds and membranes from all the fruit. Dice the apples into medium-sized chunks (after removing the peel, if you wish), and mix them with the grapefruit sections. Cut the cooked fish into small pieces and mix them with the grapefruit sections, apples, carrots, and celery.

Mix the mayonnaise, ketchup, lemon juice, cream or sour cream, and chopped nuts with a few tablespoons of the cooking liquid and a little juice from the grapefruit sections. Season this dressing with salt and pepper and mix it with the salad ingredients.

Fill the reserved grapefruit shells with the dressed fish salad. Sprinkle them with a little chopped fresh mint and top each with a cherry half if you wish.

Colin aux Cèpes

Hake with Wild Mushrooms

Serves 6

This delicate white-fleshed fish is related to cod, but in France it is considered to be in a class of its own. You may substitute any handsome, flaky, white fish, such as sole or flounder, or red snapper.

A 4-pound hake

For the court bouillon:
2 cups dry white wine
2 cups water
2 carrots, sliced
2 stalks celery, sliced
1 large onion, diced
* Bouquet garni
6 peppercorns
Pinch of saffron

1¼ pounds fresh *cèpes*, or 1 pound cultivated
    mushrooms and 1½ ounces dried *cèpes*,
    porcini, or morels
1 shallot, minced
2 tablespoons butter
½ tablespoon olive oil
1 tablespoon minced fresh tarragon
1 tablespoon minced fresh parsley

For the sauce:
½ cup dry white wine
½ cup white wine vinegar
1 clove garlic, minced
2 shallots, minced
1 tablespoon minced fresh tarragon
4 egg yolks
Salt and freshly ground pepper
¾ to 1 cup (1½ to 2 sticks) butter, melted

½ pound small shrimp, shelled
½ cup grated Gruyère cheese

To prepare the fish:
Cut the hake into steaks about 1¼ inches thick. Put all the ingredients for the court bouillon into a heavy enameled saucepan and
simmer for 20 minutes to develop the flavor. Then poach the fish
steaks in the barely simmering court bouillon until they are just
done, about 8 to 10 minutes. Set them aside in a little of the
cooking liquid to keep warm. Reserve the remaining liquid for the
sauce.

To prepare the mushrooms:
Clean the mushrooms well, trim the stems, and cut them into thin
slices. In a large skillet, sauté the shallot for 1 minute in the butter
and olive oil. Add the mushrooms, tarragon, and parsley and sauté
until the mushrooms are lightly browned, between 5 and 10 minutes. Cover them and simmer over low heat for 20 minutes. Drain
the cooked mushrooms and reserve the liquid.

To make the sauce:
Place the wine and the vinegar in a small, heavy-bottomed sauce-pan with the garlic, shallots, and tarragon. Boil over high heat to evaporate. After 5 minutes add ½ cup of the used court bouillon and 1 cup (or whatever remains) of the mushroom cooking juices. Continue cooking the sauce until it is reduced to ½ cup.

Put the egg yolks in a small, heavy saucepan. Beat in the reduced sauce and place it over medium heat. Whisk constantly until the mixture thickens. Season it to taste with salt and pepper, then add the melted butter by drops until it is all absorbed and the sauce is thick and fluffy. Keep the sauce warm.

To assemble the dish:
Place the shrimp in a saucepan with 1 cup of the court bouillon and cook them over low heat. They are done when they turn pink (about 5 minutes).

Spread the mushrooms evenly in a buttered ovenproof baking dish. Arrange the poached fish steaks on top, sprinkle with grated cheese, and brown them in a preheated 350°F oven until the cheese melts and the mushrooms are hot. Add the cooked shrimp to the sauce just before serving. Pour some sauce over the fish and serve the rest in a sauceboat.

Rendez-Vous des Primeurs

Mixed Baby Vegetables

Serves 6

This is something I like to make when my vegetable garden first begins to produce. It is just a handful of this and that, and can be varied in any way you like. However, you should use only the youngest and smallest vegetables you can find. For six people you will need about 1½ pounds of assorted vegetables.

8 scallions, trimmed and cut into 2-inch lengths on
    a sharp diagonal
1 large head broccoli, cut into flowerettes
Sugar peas
Tiny carrots, quartered and cut into 2-inch lengths
Tiny green beans
2 tablespoons butter
1 tablespoon chopped parsley
1 teaspoon chopped fresh tarragon
Salt and freshly ground pepper

Steam the scallions and broccoli flowerettes, and when they are almost done add the sugar peas. When these vegetables are just tender, remove them from the pan and refresh them in cold water.

In boiling salted water, cook the carrots, adding the beans after about a minute. Drain these vegetables and refresh them in cold water when they are cooked but still firm.

Just before serving, melt the butter in a large pan. Add all the vegetables and toss them gently to mix. Add the parsley and the tarragon, and salt and pepper to taste, and toss again. Serve as soon as the vegetables are heated through.

Fraises Cardinal

Strawberries in Raspberry Sauce

Serves 6

1½ quarts of strawberries
1 quart fresh raspberries or 2 packages frozen
    raspberries, thawed
2 tablespoons crème de cassis
3 or 4 tablespoons confectioner's sugar, or to taste

Wash the strawberries if they are sandy, and hull them. Purée the raspberries in a food processor or blender with the crème de cassis and confectioner's sugar. Strain the purée to remove the seeds. Place the strawberries in a glass bowl and pour the sauce over them so they are completely coated. Cover the bowl and chill the fruit for several hours, so the strawberries absorb the flavor of the sauce.

Variation:
Use poached peaches or pears in place of the strawberries. Assemble and serve the dish in the same manner.

TWO COUNTRY LUNCHES
À MA FAÇON

II

*Tomates aux Oeufs Pochés et Coulis
de Concombre*
Baked Eggs in Tomatoes with Cucumber Sauce

Sauté d'Agneau Printanier
Lamb Stew with New Vegetables

Fromage
Cheese
(Camembert)

Bavarois au Melon
Iced Melon Mold

Wine: A Saint-Émilion with the tomatoes and
lamb; a Muscat de Frontignan with the dessert

Tomates aux Oeufs Pochés et Coulis de Concombre

Baked Eggs in Tomatoes with Cucumber Sauce

Serves 6

6 small, firm tomatoes
6 ounces mushrooms, washed and minced
1 small onion or 2 scallions, minced
2 tablespoons butter
Salt and freshly ground pepper
6 eggs
Ground coriander
1 cucumber, peeled, seeded, and cut into pieces
1 to 2 tablespoons sour cream

Remove the tops from the tomatoes, scoop out the seeds and pulp, and drain the fruits, inverted, on paper towels. Gently sauté the minced mushrooms and onion in the butter with a little salt and pepper until they become dry.

Place the tomatoes in a buttered baking dish. Put about a tablespoon of the cooked mushroom mixture into each tomato, and break an egg in each. Sprinkle with salt, pepper, and a little ground coriander and bake in a preheated 375°F oven until the eggs are set, about 15 minutes.

Meanwhile, purée the cucumber in a food processor or blender. Season it with salt and pepper and stir in the sour cream. Serve the tomato cups hot, surrounded on the serving platter by the cold cucumber sauce.

Sauté d'Agneau Printanier

Lamb Stew with New Vegetables

Serves 6

2½ pounds boned lamb shoulder
2 tablespoons butter
2 tablespoons oil
1 tablespoon flour
1 cup dry white wine
2¼ cups water
1 tablespoon tomato paste
* Bouquet garni
2 or 3 cloves garlic
Salt and freshly ground pepper
2 zucchini, cut in ½-inch slices
⅓ to ½ pound baby carrots, peeled and quartered
½ pound frozen peas
4 ounces small pearl onions, peeled
2 teaspoons sugar
¼ cup chopped fresh parsley

Cut the lamb into 2-inch pieces, wipe it dry, and brown it in 1 tablespoon butter and the oil in a heavy casserole with a lid. Do not crowd the pieces. When all the pieces are browned, sprinkle them with flour and cook 1 minute, stirring. Moisten with the wine and 1 cup water, add the tomato paste, a large bouquet garni, garlic, salt, and pepper, and simmer, covered, over low heat or in a preheated 350°F oven for ½ hour. Add the zucchini, carrots, and peas to the casserole and simmer, covered, for an additional 30 minutes.

In a saucepan, cook the onions in 1 tablespoon butter, sugar, and 1¼ cup water, uncovered. After the water evaporates, the onions will caramelize slightly. Add them to the stew at the end of the cooking time. Correct the seasoning, sprinkle the stew with parsley, and serve it from the casserole.

Note:
This recipe is based on the traditional French way of cooking vegetables. For people who like vegetables *al dente*, reduce the final cooking time to 10 to 15 minutes.

Bavarois au Melon

Iced Melon Mold

Serves 4

The small cantaloupes from Cavaillon in the south of France that I use for this *bavarois* have a very intense flavor. Be sure to choose fully ripe melons that have a rich, strong taste.

> 2 or 3 ripe cantaloupes
> 5 tablespoons powdered sugar, or to taste
> 2 envelopes gelatin
> Juice of 1 lemon
> 4 tablespoons sweet sherry or port
> ⅓ cup heavy cream, whipped
> About 1 cup melon balls, of different colors if
>   possible (for garnish)
> Fresh mint (for garnish)

Scoop out the flesh of the cantaloupes and purée it in a food processor, blender, or food mill. Strain the purée. You should have about 3 cups. Sweeten it to taste with powdered sugar and stir well to dissolve the sugar.

Soften the gelatin in the lemon juice, adding a tablespoon or two of water if you do not have enough liquid. Heat 1 cup of the cantaloupe purée in a small saucepan. When it becomes too hot for you to dip your finger in, add the softened gelatin and stir constantly over heat for 2 minutes, or until the gelatin is completely dissolved. Add this mixture to the remaining cantaloupe purée, stirring well. Add sherry or port to taste. Chill until the mixture is thick and syrupy, then fold in the whipped cream. Pour the *bavarois* into a decorative 3½- or 4-cup mold that you have rinsed with cold water and greased with vegetable oil. Chill for at least 4 hours.

To serve, unmold the dessert onto a serving plate and garnish it with melon balls doused in a little more sherry or port and with sprigs of fresh mint.

BUFFET AROUND THE POOL

Homard Froid à la Mayonnaise au Gingembre
Cold Lobster with Ginger Mayonnaise

Filet de Boeuf en Gelée
Cold Roast Fillet of Beef with Aspic

Salade de Petits Pois Frais
Minted Pea Salad

Fromage
Cheese (Grand Brie or Muenster)

Tartes aux Amandes et aux Framboises
Raspberry-Almond Tarts

Wine: A Pouilly-Fumé with the lobster, then a
red Burgundy, perhaps a Santenay

One of the greatest charms of Normandy is that it is so close to Paris. Many Parisians delight in finding a dilapidated old manor house and transforming it into something much more colorful and charming than the original. In Normandy these Parisians enjoy healthy, restful weekends and, during the month of August, the ritual of daily parties.

Swimming pools are something the average Norman regards as altogether curious, feeling that enough water comes from the rain. To Normans the idea of looking at water, let alone swimming in it, is anything but appealing. But to those who have brought the manor houses back to life, a buffet around the pool is a delightful way to entertain. Everyone has a chance to admire the house and the lovely woodland garden that usually surrounds it.

Homard Froid à la Mayonnaise au Gingembre

Cold Lobster with Ginger Mayonnaise

Serves 6

Lobster simply cooked (we often poach it in sea water) and served with freshly made mayonnaise is one of the great delicacies of summer.

For the mayonnaise:
2 egg yolks, warmed
½ teaspoon grated lemon zest
1 tablespoon lemon juice
1 to 1¼ cups vegetable oil
1½ teaspoons grated fresh ginger root
Salt and freshly ground white pepper
Cream (optional)

For the court bouillon:
Water
Salt
2 or 3 sprigs thyme
2 or 3 sprigs tarragon or fresh fennel
1 bay leaf

3 lobsters, 1½ pounds each
A 3-inch piece of fresh ginger root
Watercress (for garnish)

To make the mayonnaise:
Beat the egg yolks and lemon zest with the lemon juice in a food processor or with an electric mixer. Add the oil very slowly, by drops. When the mayonnaise has thickened, add the ginger and flavor to taste with salt and pepper, adding more lemon juice if

you wish. You may thin the mayonnaise with a little cream. It will keep for several days in the refrigerator if you cover it.

To make the court bouillon:
Bring a large amount of salted water to a boil in a large pot with a cover. Add the herbs and simmer for 15 minutes.

To cook and prepare the lobsters:
Return the court bouillon to a boil, plunge the lobsters into the pot, cover, and simmer for about 12 minutes. Remove the pot from the heat and let the lobsters cool in the liquid. (You may cook the lobsters a day in advance and refrigerate them.)

When the lobsters are cool, split each one lengthwise down the back, using a strong, sharp-pointed knife. Discard the dark intestinal veins. Remove the claws and separate the tails from the chests. Keeping the tail shells intact, remove the meat from the tails and the bodies; slice it and return it to the shells. Remove the meat from the claws and reserve it whole.

Trim the piece of ginger root into a rectangle, then cut it lengthwise into very thin slices. Then cut the slices into fine strips.

To serve:
Pour a ribbon of mayonnaise across the sliced lobster meat in the tail shells. Place a pink claw on top and garnish with the julienne strips of fresh ginger root. Line a serving plate with watercress, put the lobster tails on it, and chill until serving time. Serve the remaining mayonnaise in a sauceboat.

Filet de Boeuf en Gelée

Cold Roast Fillet of Beef with Aspic

Serves 6

This is a festive dish, and much easier to prepare than the usual cold braised beef. It is best made a day in advance.

> Larding fat or strips of bacon
> A 3-pound fillet of beef, trimmed, cut from the
>   large end of the tenderloin
> Salt and freshly ground pepper
>
> *For the aspic:*
> * 3 cups clear beef stock, or 2 large beef bouillon
>   cubes suitable for 4 cups bouillon, dissolved
>   in 3 cups water
> 2 envelopes gelatin
> ½ cup Madeira
> Parsley (for garnish)

Preheat the oven to 475°F. Tie the larding fat or strips of bacon on top of the roast and season it with salt and pepper. Place the meat on a rack in a roasting pan, put it in the oven, and immediately reduce the heat to 350°F. Roast to an internal temperature of 120°F as shown on a meat thermometer, about 20 to 25 minutes for rare meat. Remove the beef from the oven and let it stand for ½ hour. Remove the fat or bacon strips, then place the beef in the refrigerator.

To make the aspic, bring the stock to a simmer. Soften the gelatin in the Madeira and dissolve it in the hot stock. Strain the aspic and chill it in a shallow pan until it is set, about 2 hours. Then dice it into ½-inch pieces.

To serve the roast, carve it, then arrange a layer of aspic cubes on a serving platter. Place overlapping slices of meat down the center and surround them with more aspic. Garnish with a small bouquet of parsley at each end of the platter. (Cooked baby carrots dipped in aspic are also attractive.) Store the beef in the refrigerator until you are ready to serve it.

Salade de Petits Pois Frais

Minted Pea Salad

Serves 6

3 cups tiny new peas, fresh or frozen
* ½ cup mayonnaise
* ½ cup *crème fraîche* or sour cream
1 tablespoon Dijon mustard
½ cup chopped fresh mint
2 tablespoons chopped fresh chives
Boston lettuce
Mint leaves (for garnish)
Cherry tomatoes (for garnish)

Cook the peas, uncovered, in boiling salted water until they are barely tender. Immediately refresh them in cold water, and drain. Combine the mayonnaise, *crème fraîche* or sour cream, and mustard and pour them over the peas. Add the mint and chives and toss gently to coat the peas with the dressing. Serve on Boston lettuce and garnish with whole mint leaves and halved cherry tomatoes.

Tartes aux Amandes et aux Framboises

Raspberry-Almond Tarts

Serves 6

For the tart shells:
¾ cup almonds
1 cup flour
2 tablespoons sugar
½ teaspoon salt
6 tablespoons cold unsalted butter, cut in 8 pieces
1 large egg, beaten

For the filling:
2½ cups whole raspberries
About 1 cup red raspberry jelly
Lemon juice

Using a food processor with the steel blade in place, grind the almonds. Add the flour, sugar, and salt, and mix well. Then add the pieces of butter and mix until the dough is crumbly. With the processor running, add the egg through the feed tube. Stop the machine when the dough begins to form a ball. (You may make the pastry by hand, following the instructions for *Pâte Brisée*, p. 256, or *Pâte Sucrée*, p. 260.) Chill.

To make the tart shells, divide the chilled dough into eight portions. Shape each portion into a ball and roll it into a 4½- to 5-inch circle. Fit the circles into 3½- to 4-inch tart pans, prick well, and chill about half an hour. Bake the shells in a preheated 400°F oven until they are lightly browned, about 12 minutes, and cool before filling.

Wash the berries. Melt the jelly in a saucepan and thin it with lemon juice to taste. Fill the tart shells with berries and brush them with the jelly glaze. These tarts are best if served within a few hours.

Variations:

You may use other fruits — strawberries, peaches, or quince — in the same manner. You may also substitute currant jelly for the raspberry jelly.

A PARISIAN-STYLE JUNE LUNCH

IV

Potage Germiny
Cream of Sorrel Soup

Turbot Farci, Sauce Champagne
Stuffed Turbot with Champagne Sauce

Pommes de Terre Maître d'Hôtel
Steamed Potatoes with Herb Butter

Salade de Saison
Mixed Green Salad

Pyramide de Framboises Isabelle
Pyramid of Raspberries

Wine: A Champagne Blanc de Blancs, such as an
Avize, with the whole menu

June is the month for entertaining in Paris. The Grand Prix horse races take place at Chantilly and Longchamps, the tennis championships are held at Roland Garros, and the English Embassy has its annual garden party. In July Parisians resume more casual parties, on the terrace if possible, and in August everyone leaves the city for vacations in the outlying regions.

I have delightful memories of serving this June luncheon. It is stylish but not at all complicated. I have named the dessert for my sister, Isabelle, who used to be lost behind pyramids of raspberries and black currants on market days in the neighboring town of Yvetot. Isabelle loves to garden, and a few years ago she decided that it would be fun to have a berry farm at La Coquetterie. She thought that the farmer's children could pick the berries for pocket money and that she would then sell the fruit at the market. It never occurred to her that she might not sell all the berries. On days when Isabelle and the children returned home from the market with unsold berries she could not bear to throw them away, and so she learned to make jam. The berry farm is a thing of the past, but, I am happy to say, Isabelle continues to make excellent jam.

Potage Germiny

Cream of Sorrel Soup

Serves 8 to 10

> 6 ounces fresh sorrel, with stems removed
> 2 tablespoons butter
> * 2 quarts well-flavored stock or consommé
> 4 egg yolks
> ¾ cup cream
> Chopped chervil (for garnish)
> ⅓ cup port wine (if you are serving the soup cold)

Wash and dry the sorrel. Holding the leaves in bunches, cut across them in thin slices. Cook the sorrel in butter in a large saucepan over low heat, stirring, until it "melts" or is reduced by half and turns a paler color. Add the stock and simmer for 15 minutes.

Mix the egg yolks and cream in a large bowl. Just before serving, pour the hot soup into the egg-and-cream mixture, whisking vigorously. Then pour the mixture back into the saucepan and cook it gently over medium heat, stirring constantly, until it coats the back of a spoon (as for a custard), about 5 minutes. Sprinkle the soup with chopped chervil before serving.

To serve this soup cold, chill the mixture and add the port just before serving.

Variation:
Potage aux Herbes Aromatiques (Fresh Herb Soup): Substitute 6 ounces of mixed fresh herbs of your choice, such as tarragon, chives, and chervil, for the sorrel.

Turbot Farci, Sauce Champagne

Stuffed Turbot with Champagne Sauce

Serves 8

A 4-pound turbot or sea bass

For the fish stock:
Bones from the fish
1 carrot
1 onion
1 shallot
2 tablespoons butter
1 cup white wine
2 cups water
* Bouquet garni
6 peppercorns

For the mousseline:
1 pound boneless fillets of red snapper, salmon, scrod, haddock, or any other fish
1 small red bell pepper
1 or 2 egg whites
* ¾ to 1¼ cups *crème fraîche* or heavy cream
Salt and freshly ground pepper
Nutmeg
Cayenne

2 to 3 shallots, minced
½ bottle champagne
* ¼ cup *crème fraîche* or heavy cream

Ask the market to bone the turbot, leaving it whole. Keep the bones. If you bone the fish yourself, use the same method as for *Poisson Farci au Cidre* (p. 193).

To make the stock:
Sauté the bones and vegetables in the butter in a saucepan until they begin to brown. Add the wine, water, bouquet garni, and peppercorns. Simmer, uncovered, for 20 minutes, then strain, return to the saucepan, and reduce the stock by half to concentrate the flavor.

To make the mousseline:
Cut the fish fillets into chunks and purée them with the red pepper in a blender or food processor until smooth. Add 1 egg white and ¾ cup *crème fraîche* or cream. Season with salt, pepper, nutmeg, and cayenne to taste. Poach a spoonful of the mousseline in the simmering fish stock or in simmering salted water and check the seasoning and consistency. If the mixture is too soft, add the remaining egg white; if it is too dense, add more cream. Correct the seasoning if necessary.

To assemble the dish:
Sprinkle the cavity of the turbot with salt and pepper and fill it with the mousseline mixture. Place the fish on its side in a buttered baking dish, sprinkle with minced shallots, cover with champagne, and bake it in a preheated 350°F oven until it is done and flakes easily, about 1 hour. Cover it with foil if the fish becomes dry on top.

When the fish is done, remove it and keep it warm. Strain its cooking liquid into the fish stock. Add the remaining ¼ cup *crème fraîche* or cream and reduce the liquid by half. To serve, coat the fish with a little sauce, and pass the remainder in a separate dish.

Pommes de Terre Maître d'Hôtel

Steamed Potatoes with Herb Butter

Serves 6

3 pounds small potatoes, peeled
1 tablespoon minced fresh parsley
1 tablespoon minced fresh chives, tarragon, and
    thyme
6 to 8 tablespoons butter, melted
Salt and freshly ground pepper
Juice of 1 lemon, or to taste

Steam the potatoes until they are tender. Place them in a pan with
the herbs and melted butter; toss gently to coat well. You may
keep them warm for about ½ hour before serving. Season to taste
with salt, pepper, and lemon juice.

Pyramide de Framboises Isabelle

Pyramid of Raspberries

Serves 8

Several large flat maple, oak, or grape leaves
1½ to 2 quarts fresh raspberries
Powdered sugar
* 2 cups *crème fraîche* or lightly whipped cream

Wipe the leaves off and place them on a round silver or glass
serving tray with a rim. Arrange the raspberries in the center,
piling them carefully as high as possible in a pyramid shape. Just
before serving dust them with powdered sugar, and serve them
with a bowl of *crème fraîche* or lightly whipped cream.

A SMART LUNCH FOR FRIENDS
EN ROUTE TO DEAUVILLE

Soupe Glacée à la Laitue
Cold Cream of Lettuce Soup

Poulet en Chaud-Froid à l'Estragon
Cold Chicken with Tarragon Cream Jelly

Salade de Haricots Verts
Green Bean Salad with Tarragon

Fromage
Cheese (Pont-l'Évêque)

Tarte aux Fraises
Strawberry Tart

Wine: Champagne with the whole menu

Located some miles west of Honfleur and close to the estuary of the Seine, Deauville is less than an hour's drive from La Coquetterie, thanks to the bridge of Tancarville. The magnificent view from the bridge, which is one of the highest and longest in Europe, is not the least of the pleasures along the road for friends who stop at La Coquetterie on their way to Deauville.

August in Deauville is a horse-lover's paradise. The beaches of this old-fashioned seaside resort are all but forgotten as crowds flock to the international yearling sales, the annual world champion polo matches, and the running of the Deauville Grand Prix.

En route to Deauville, friends arrive at La Coquetterie bubbling with anticipation. As much as they enjoy the pleasures of the country, it lacks the excitement the thoroughbreds promise, and they are eager to be on their way. On these occasions I like the table set under the trees and a light, sophisticated menu that will leave my guests in high spirits. Of course I choose a Pont-l'Évêque for the cheese, because the nice little city for which the cheese is named is only a few kilometers from Deauville.

Soupe Glacée à la Laitue

Cold Cream of Lettuce Soup

Serves 6

2 or 3 well-washed leeks, white part only
1 bunch watercress, leaves and tender stems only
1 large head Boston lettuce
3 tablespoons butter
1½ cups peas, fresh or frozen
1 tablespoon chopped fresh tarragon
* 5 cups chicken or veal stock
1 cup heavy cream
Salt and freshly ground white pepper

Chop the leeks and the watercress. You should have about 3 cups of watercress. Shred the lettuce; you should have about 4½ cups. Reserve about ¼ cup for the garnish.

Heat the butter in a large, heavy saucepan, add the leeks, and sauté them until soft. Add the watercress, lettuce, peas, and tarragon, together with 1 cup of the chicken or veal stock. Cook, partially covered, over low heat for about 20 minutes.

Purée the cooked vegetables in a food processor or blender. Strain them into a large bowl; add the remaining stock and the cream. Season to taste with salt and pepper. Chill the soup, covered, for several hours.

Serve the soup garnished with lettuce shredded as fine as possible. You may also serve it hot.

Poulet en Chaud-Froid à l'Estragon

Cold Chicken with Tarragon Cream Jelly

Serves 6

2 chickens, 3 pounds each
Salt and freshly ground pepper
A bunch of fresh tarragon
3 carrots, coarsely chopped
2 leeks, chopped
1 tablespoon butter
5 peppercorns
* Bouquet garni made with tarragon sprigs
* 5 cups chicken stock, or water and bouillon cubes
Gelatin
Egg whites (3 per quart of cooking liquid)
¼ to ½ cup heavy cream or *crème fraîche

Wipe the chickens, removing the necks and giblets and reserving them for another recipe. Salt and pepper the interiors and insert a few large sprigs of tarragon. Truss the birds and set them aside.

In a heavy pot, brown the carrots and leeks in the butter with the peppercorns, a little salt, and the bouquet garni. After a few minutes, add the stock or water and bouillon cubes and simmer ½ hour.

Place the trussed chickens in the broth, cover, and simmer for 35 or 40 minutes, until the birds are done. Remove them to a cool place and leave them to cool completely.

Measure the stock; you will need 1 envelope of gelatin for every 2 cups of cooking liquid. Soften as much gelatin as you need in ⅓ cup of cold stock or water, then dissolve it in the hot cooking liquid. Test the stock for the correct amount of gelatin by placing a little on a plate and refrigerating it. If it doesn't jell in a short time, add a little more gelatin or boil the stock down further. Taste the sample for seasoning while it is cold.

Add a few fresh sprigs of tarragon to the stock, boil for several minutes, and remove the sprigs. Whisk as many egg whites as you need and pour them into the hot stock, stirring rapidly. When the stock comes back to the boil, reduce the heat, stop stirring, and allow the stock to clarify for 10 or 15 minutes. Make a small hole in the side of the forming crust, to let steam out and to allow you to watch the clarification. Strain the stock gently and set it aside to cool.

When the clarified chicken broth is nearly cold but not yet completely jelled, mix in the heavy cream or *crème fraîche*. Correct the seasoning and continue to cool. Just before serving, add 2 or 3 tablespoons of finely chopped tarragon leaves.

When the chicken is cold, cut it into eight serving pieces and remove the skin. Place on a grill over a tray and top with the tarragon cream jelly. Cover well and refrigerate until you are ready to serve. Then place the chicken pieces on a deep platter and surround them with the remaining jelly.

Salade de Haricots Verts

Green Bean Salad with Tarragon

Serves 6

2½ pounds green beans (the smallest you can find),
    washed and with the ends snapped off
Boston or Bibb lettuce
Red chicory
Strips of pimento (optional)
½ cup chopped walnuts

For the vinaigrette:
¼ cup walnut oil
⅓ cup vegetable oil
Juice of 1 lime or ½ lemon
½ teaspoon dry mustard
1 tablespoon minced fresh tarragon
Salt and freshly ground pepper

Cook the beans in a large quantity of boiling, heavily salted water until tender, about 8 to 12 minutes. Drain them and refresh under cold water, then spread them on a towel to dry. You may cook the beans a day ahead and keep them covered in the refrigerator.

Cover a salad plate with Boston or Bibb lettuce, then arrange some leaves of red chicory and the green beans on top. You may "tie" the beans in bunches with strips of pimento. Sprinkle the salad lightly with chopped walnuts.

Just before serving, place all the ingredients for the vinaigrette in a cruet or jar and shake them together until they are mixed. Drizzle the dressing over the salad.

Tarte aux Fraises

Strawberry Tart

Serves 6

The berries in this tart stand on their own with no custard, but they must be perfectly ripe.

* * ¾ **pound leftover puff pastry or demi-puff pastry**
* 1 **quart fresh strawberries**
* ½ **cup strawberry or red currant jelly**
* **Lemon juice**
* * 2 **cups** *crème fraîche* **or lightly whipped cream**

Roll the leftover pastry about ¼-inch thick and with it line a 10-inch tart pan that has a removable bottom. Prick the bottom well and chill for 1 hour. Bake the shell in a preheated 350°F oven until golden, about 25 to 30 minutes. If the shell has risen, press it down while it is warm. Cool it on a rack and remove the outside ring of the pan.

Wash and hull the berries. Dry them well.

Not more than 2 hours before serving, arrange the berries in the tart shell. Brush them with jelly melted in a saucepan and thinned with a little lemon juice, if necessary. Serve the tart with a bowl of *crème fraîche* or lightly whipped cream.

AUTUMN

Four Menus to Please Hunting Friends
Three Festive Autumn Menus
Two Dinners by the Fire
A Dinner from La Bastide du Roy

In October the air in Normandy is filled with the smell of freshly plowed fields, the green woods turn to scarlet and gold, and *la cueillette des pommes*, the apple harvest, begins. Hunting parties at La Coquetterie bring everyone together in a special kind of comradeship as the hunters share the last days of good weather while shooting. They require a hearty breakfast, and between one and two o'clock we serve a light lunch in the field, while they give their dogs a rest. There is plenty of tea and coffee to warm everyone up, and little sandwiches, red wine, and fruit.

By five-thirty the countryside is dark and everyone has returned to La Coquetterie for the presentation of the birds. Pheasant, partridge, and duck are arranged on the grass in an elaborate still life, and the gamekeeper formally reads off the day's tally. Later in the evening our guests sit by the fire, sharing hunting stories or solving the problems of the world. Dinner is usually the best part of the party, and although it is served at an early hour, guests always stay quite late.

But the pleasures of autumn do not belong only to the hunters. The season's bounty is shared by us all. Markets are filled with mountains of red and yellow Reine des Reinettes apples, orange pumpkins, and great green cabbages, and baskets of wild mushrooms begin to appear. Chestnuts are harvested, our apples are pressed for sparkling cider, and the kitchen is filled with the fragrance of my sister Isabelle's steaming kettles of apple jelly.

These glorious days reflect the calm before the winter storms, which send people rushing to shutter their houses and depart with the swallows. Weekend parties go on through the fall season at the château, but they are less frequent and more intimate. Autumn is a time for good-byes—but only for short ones, for at Easter our friends return to open their houses, plant their gardens, and prepare for summer again.

FOUR MENUS TO
PLEASE HUNTING FRIENDS

These menus contain first courses of character followed by game birds or meat to be eaten with pleasure. Hearty but not rustic, this country fare can be just as successful with nonhunting friends in the city.

I

Beignets de Crevettes, Sauce Tartare
Shrimp Fritters with Tartare Sauce

Perdreaux au Calvados et aux Raisins
Partridge with Calvados and Grapes

Purée de Betteraves
Purée of Beets

Salade de Saison
Mixed Green Salad

Sorbet aux Quatre Fruits
Four Fruit Sorbet

Wine: A Chablis with the first course, then a
Bordeaux Pauillac

Beignets de Crevettes, Sauce Tartare

Shrimp Fritters with Tartare Sauce

Serves 6

For the fritters:
1 package active dry yeast
2 tablespoons warm water
1 cup flour
2 egg yolks
4 tablespoons tepid milk
Salt
2 egg whites, beaten until stiff
Oil
30 freshly cooked shrimp (about 2 pounds), shelled
    and deveined
¼ cup chopped parsley (for garnish)

For the sauce:
3 hard-boiled egg yolks
1 tablespoon Dijon mustard
White wine vinegar
Salt and freshly ground pepper
1 cup oil
2 to 4 tablespoons mixed fresh chervil, tarragon,
    and chives
1 tablespoon chopped parsley
2 tablespoons minced sour pickle
3 or 4 tablespoons capers
2 or 3 sieved hard-boiled egg whites (optional)
Few drops of Tabasco sauce (optional)

To make the fritters:
Dissolve the yeast in the warm water. In a mixing bowl, combine
the flour, yeast, egg yolks, 2 tablespoons of the milk, and salt to

taste. Beat with a wooden spoon until smooth. Let the batter stand for at least 30 minutes, then fold in the egg whites and the remaining 2 tablespoons of milk.

In a heavy pan, heat enough oil to deep-fry the shrimp until it reaches 375°F on a frying thermometer. Place the shrimp in the batter and mix gently, then fry a few batter-coated shrimp at a time until they are golden and puffed. Drain them on paper towels.

To make the sauce:
Mash the egg yolks with the mustard and vinegar. Add a little salt and freshly ground pepper. Proceed as with a regular mayonnaise (p. 252), adding the oil slowly as you whisk constantly. Then add the herbs, pickle, and capers, and the egg whites and Tabasco sauce if you wish. Correct the seasoning to taste.

To serve:
Place the fritters on a hot serving plate, sprinkle them with parsley, and pass the *sauce Tartare* in a separate dish.

Perdreaux au Calvados et aux Raisins

Partridge with Calvados and Grapes

Serves 6

The young partridges called for in this recipe are named *perdreaux*; older birds are *perdrix*. You may substitute Cornish game hens for the partridges.

> 3 pounds large seedless grapes, peeled
> ½ teaspoon crushed peppercorns
> ½ cup plus 3 tablespoons Calvados
> 1 cup plain yogurt
> 6 partridges
> Salt and freshly ground pepper
> 12 slices bacon
> 6 tablespoons butter
> 2 carrots, diced
> 4 large shallots, chopped
> * Bouquet garni
> * 3 cups chicken stock
> 1 tablespoon flour

Mix the grapes, crushed peppercorns, and ½ cup Calvados in a bowl and macerate for 1 hour. Then combine 1½ cups of the macerated grapes with the yogurt.

Wash and pat dry the partridges, then stuff them with the grape-yogurt mixture. Truss the birds and rub their skins with salt and pepper. Lay 2 bacon slices over each breast and secure them with string.

Melt 4 tablespoons of butter in a heavy skillet and brown the birds on all sides. Remove them from the skillet. In the same butter, brown the carrots and shallots. Put the vegetables in a large casserole, add the bouquet garni, and place the birds on top. Pour in the chicken stock, cover the casserole, and bake it in a preheated 350°F oven for 40 minutes, or until the birds are tender.

Five minutes before the partridges are done, add the remaining grapes to the skillet, flame them with the 3 tablespoons of Calvados, and cook until heated through. In a separate bowl, prepare a *beurre manié* by combining the flour and the 2 remaining tablespoons of butter and mixing until they are smooth.

Transfer the partridges to a warm serving platter, remove the trussing strings, and keep them warm. Reduce the liquid in which they cooked by one-third. Thicken it with the *beurre manié* as needed and boil this sauce for 1 or 2 minutes. Correct the seasoning and strain. To serve, surround the partridges with the grape mixture and pour the sauce over them.

Purée de Betteraves

Purée of Beets

Serves 6

3 pounds fresh beets
* ¾ cup *crème fraîche* or heavy cream
½ small onion, grated
Few drops of sherry vinegar or lemon juice
Salt and freshly ground pepper

Wash the beets and cook them in a baking dish in a preheated 350°F oven for 40 minutes or until they are tender. Peel them and cut them into large pieces with a stainless-steel knife. Purée the cooked beets in a food processor or blender, or put them through a food mill. Add the *crème fraîche* or cream and grated onion and season to taste with sherry vinegar, salt, and pepper. You may serve the purée hot or cold, but if you reheat it, do not boil it. If you serve it cold, beat it well before serving.

Sorbet aux Quatre Fruits

Four Fruit Sorbet

Serves 6 to 8

4 pounds bananas
1 large or 2 small pineapples
2 oranges
2 lemons
1 cup confectioner's sugar, or to taste
1 egg white

Peel the bananas and pineapple and cut them into chunks. Peel and section the oranges and lemons, retaining the juice. In a food processor or blender, purée the fruits with the sugar, adding more sugar to taste, if you wish. Transfer the puréed fruits into a large, flat metal dish and freeze until the sorbet is almost frozen but still a little slushy. Then beat the mixture until fluffy in a food processor or with an electric mixer. Add the egg white and continue beating 1 minute. Return the sorbet to the freezer.

To make additional volume, beat the refrozen mixture again before serving or refreezing. After beating it for the last time, put it in an ice-cream mold or freezer container. Keep it in the freezer until you are ready to serve it.

FOUR MENUS TO PLEASE HUNTING FRIENDS

II

Filets de Poisson Antillaise
Fish Fillets with Peppers and Bananas

Selle d'Agneau Armenonville
Roast Saddle of Lamb

Aubergines Sydney
Eggplant-Stuffed Tomatoes

Fromage
Cheese (Gaperon)

Bavarois Praliné
Cold Praline Soufflé

Wine: A Sauterne with the first course and the dessert,
a Saint-Julien with the *Selle d'Agneau*

Filets de Poisson Antillaise

Fish Fillets with Peppers and Bananas

Serves 6

3 red bell peppers
Oil
4 tablespoons butter
2 bananas
6 fish fillets (red snapper, bass, or bluefish)
Salt and freshly ground pepper
1 tablespoon very finely chopped parsley (for garnish)
2 lemons, thinly sliced (for garnish)

To roast the peppers, pull off their stems, cut each one in half lengthwise, and remove the seeds. Place them skin side up in a shallow roasting pan and sprinkle with oil, then put them under the broiler and grill for about 15 minutes, until the peppers are black and blistered. Remove them from the broiler and enclose them in a plastic bag until they are cool enough to handle. The humidity in the bag helps to loosen the skins, which you should be able to pull off easily as soon as the peppers are cool.

Slice the peeled, roasted peppers into strips and drain them well on paper towels. Sauté the pepper strips lightly in 1 tablespoon of butter, drain, and arrange them in a thin layer on a warmed serving platter. Keep them warm.

Peel the bananas, cut them into ⅓-inch slices, and set them aside. Season the fish fillets with salt and pepper. Melt 2 tablespoons of butter in a large skillet and sauté the fish quickly, but do not brown it. Arrange the fillets on top of the peppers on the platter and keep them warm.

Lightly sauté the bananas for several minutes in the hot butter in which you cooked the fish. Remove the bananas from the skillet with a slotted spoon and arrange them around the fish.

Add 1 tablespoon of butter to the skillet and cook until very hot but not brown. Pour this over the fish, bananas, and pepper strips. Sprinkle the dish with the chopped parsley and arrange the lemon slices down the middle of the platter. Serve at once.

Selle d'Agneau Armenonville

Roast Saddle of Lamb

Serves 6

A saddle of lamb, 4 to 6 pounds
¼ cup fresh bread crumbs
2 tablespoons finely chopped parsley
½ tablespoon finely chopped garlic
1½ tablespoons finely chopped shallots
3 ounces butter, cooked to a light brown
* 1¾ cups brown stock
Salt and freshly ground pepper
Cold butter (optional)

Remove the kidneys and most of the fat from the underside of the saddle of lamb. Flatten the side flaps of meat and fold them tightly under the saddle. Tie the lamb snugly, then roast it in a preheated 425°F oven for about 30 minutes.

While the meat is cooking, mix together the bread crumbs, parsley, garlic, and shallots. After the lamb has cooked for ½ hour, remove it from the oven and increase the oven heat to 475°F. Cover the top of the lamb with the bread-crumb mixture and drizzle the melted butter and about ½ cup of the stock over it. Roast the lamb for 10 minutes more, then move it to a warm serving platter.

Pour off the grease from the roasting pan and deglaze the pan with the remaining stock. Bring the liquid to a boil, scraping the bottom of the pan well to loosen all the congealed meat juices.

Reduce the sauce to 1 cup, add salt and pepper if they are needed, and if you wish, whisk in some cold butter chunks. Strain the sauce immediately and serve it in a sauceboat.

Note:
For a 6-pound saddle, count 40 minutes' cooking time at 425°F, instead of 30 minutes.

Aubergines Sydney

Eggplant-Stuffed Tomatoes

Serves 6

6 medium tomatoes
Salt and freshly ground pepper
5 medium eggplants
Olive oil or vegetable oil
1 or 2 cloves garlic, minced
About 1 teaspoon mixed dried thyme, marjoram,
and savory
½ cup grated Swiss cheese

Cut the top quarter off each of the tomatoes, scoop out the insides, and invert the tomatoes on paper towels to drain for 10 minutes. Then sprinkle the cavities with salt and pepper and bake the tomatoes for 10 minutes in a preheated 350°F oven.

Peel the eggplants and slice them lengthwise into ⅜-inch slices. Sprinkle the slices with oil, salt, and pepper, and broil them until they are soft and browned, about 10 minutes on each side. Chop the cooked eggplants into small pieces.

In a medium-sized bowl, soften the garlic in a little olive or vegetable oil. Stir in the chopped cooked eggplant, dried herbs, and additional salt and pepper if necessary. Divide the eggplant mixture evenly among the tomatoes, stuff each tomato cup with its share, and top with grated Swiss cheese. Run the tomatoes under the broiler for a few minutes to brown the cheese.

Bavarois Praliné

Cold Praline Soufflé

Serves 8 to 10

½ cup caramelized almonds, finely ground, or ⅓
    cup ground nut brittle, plus 2 to 3 tablespoons
    (for garnish)
2 envelopes gelatin
1 cup strong black coffee
3 cups milk
9 egg yolks
1 cup plus 1 tablespoon sugar
1 teaspoon vanilla extract
9 egg whites
Pinch of salt
1 cup whipped cream

To make caramelized almonds:
In a saucepan, moisten ¼ cup sugar with 1 tablespoon water. Cook over high heat until the syrup is light brown. Add ½ cup of blanched almonds and continue cooking until the syrup is medium brown. Spread the mixture on a lightly greased cookie sheet to harden.

To make the soufflé:
Soften the gelatin in the warm coffee. In a large saucepan, bring the milk to a boil. Set it aside.

In a large bowl, beat the egg yolks and the cup of sugar until they are fluffy and light in color. Pour the cooled milk slowly into the egg-yolk mixture, whisking constantly. Then pour the liquid back into the saucepan and cook over medium heat, stirring constantly, until the mixture coats the back of a spoon. Add the vanilla and the coffee-gelatin mixture and stir well to dissolve the gelatin. Remove the mixture from the heat.

In a chilled bowl, beat the egg whites with a pinch of salt until they form soft peaks. Add the remaining tablespoon of sugar and continue beating until the whites form stiff peaks. Fold the egg whites gently into the custard mixture and set it in the refrigerator to cool. Stir it gently once or twice to keep it from separating.

When the mixture has almost set, fold in the whipped cream and ground caramelized almonds or nut brittle. Pour the soufflé into a decorative 6- or 8-cup mold that you have rinsed out with cold water and chill it for at least 5 hours, until it has completely set.

To serve the soufflé, dip the mold briefly in hot water to loosen the dessert and invert it onto a serving platter. Decorate it with crushed nuts or nut brittle.

FOUR MENUS TO PLEASE HUNTING FRIENDS

III

Mousse de Lotte au Safran
Anglerfish Mousse with Saffron

Cailles aux Figues Fraîches et au Miel
Quail in Honey Sauce with Fresh Figs

Purée de Poireaux
Leek Purée

Salade de Saison
Mixed Green Salad

Tarte Chaude aux Pommes
Apple-Almond Puff Pastry Tart

Wine: A Sylvaner with the fish, then a
Saint-Émilion

Mousse de Lotte au Safran

Anglerfish Mousse with Saffron

Serves 4 to 6

1 pound anglerfish, cleaned and boned (you may
    use monkfish or any other large, firm-fleshed
    white fish)
Salt and freshly ground pepper
Saffron threads
2 eggs
2 tablespoons heavy cream
2 pounds fresh spinach
1 tablespoon butter

Cut the fish into chunks and purée them in a blender or food
processor. Season with salt and pepper. In a very small saucepan,
add a few threads of saffron to 3 or 4 tablespoons of water; bring
it to a boil, then set it aside to cool.

Add 2 tablespoons of the cooled saffron water to the fish purée,
reserving the rest. Then add the eggs and cream. Beat the mixture
well and taste; correct the seasoning, adding more saffron if necessary.

Wash the spinach, remove the stems, and pick it over, separating the largest and best leaves from the rest. Blanch as many leaves
as you will need to wrap around 4 to 6 portions of fish mousse.
Refresh the leaves in cold water and drain them on paper towels.
Arrange them in 4 to 6 small groups and divide the mousse mixture among them, placing several spoonfuls in the center of each
group of leaves. Wrap the spinach leaves around the mixture,
making sure that you seal each package well. Steam the packages
for 15 to 20 minutes, until they are done.

Alternative method: Place the blanched, refreshed, and drained spinach leaves in a well-buttered ring mold. Be sure to cover the inside and have the leaves extend over the sides of the mold. Fill the mold with the mousse, then fold over the extending spinach leaves to cover and enclose the mousse. Place the mold in a water bath and bring it to a boil on top of the stove. Then transfer it to a preheated 350°F oven and bake until it is set, about 20 minutes.

Cook the remaining spinach in boiling salted water until it is just done. Refresh it in cold water, drain, and chop it into fine pieces. In a skillet, heat the butter over medium-high heat; rapidly sauté the chopped spinach. Season it with salt and pepper.

To serve, place the mousse in the center of a warmed platter and surround it with the cooked chopped spinach.

Cailles aux Figues Fraîches et au Miel

Quail in Honey Sauce with Fresh Figs

Serves 6

12 small quail
Salt and freshly ground pepper
Thyme
2 tablespoons butter
1 cup sweet white wine, preferably Sauterne or
    Sherry
12 fresh figs
1 to 2 tablespoons honey
Lemon juice
Arrowroot or cornstarch

Sprinkle the quail, inside and out, with salt, pepper, and thyme. Truss the birds, if you wish.

In a heavy skillet, heat the butter over medium-high heat and sauté the quail for a few minutes on each side. Transfer them to a preheated 400°F oven and finish cooking them for about 15 minutes. The birds should be slightly pink when you remove them to a heated serving platter. Cover and keep them warm.

Pour off any excess fat from the skillet, then deglaze it with the wine and reduce the liquid for 1 minute. Add the figs and cook 5 minutes. Season the sauce to taste with salt, pepper, honey, and lemon juice. If you wish to thicken the sauce, mix a little arrowroot or cornstarch in some cold wine or water and add it to the hot sauce. Correct the seasoning.

Remove the figs from the sauce and arrange them around the quail on the serving platter, then strain the sauce over the quail. Serve at once.

Purée de Poireaux

Leek Purée

Serves 6

1½ pounds young leeks
3 tablespoons butter
½ cup cream, or to taste
Salt and freshly ground pepper

To wash the leeks, cut off the root end and about half to two-thirds of the green part of each one. Starting about 2 inches from the root, slice upward through the green tips. Rotate the vegetable ninety degrees and make another cut so that all but the bottom is cut in quarters lengthwise. Rinse the leeks well under cold running water, as they are often sandy. Cut the washed leeks into roughly 2-inch pieces.

Steam the leeks for about 45 minutes, until they are very soft, then sauté them in butter. Purée the cooked leeks in a food mill.

(A food processor or a blender is much less effective than a food mill in removing the filaments from the leeks, but you can use one. Just strain the leeks before adding the cream and seasonings.) Put them in a saucepan, return them to a low heat, and add cream and seasonings to taste. Heat the mixture thoroughly. You may make the purée ahead of time and reheat it just before serving.

Tarte Chaude aux Pommes

Apple-Almond Puff Pastry Tart

You will find a different type of apple tart in almost every little town in Normandy. This is the one we make at La Coquetterie.

* * ¾ **pound puff pastry**
* **2 pounds apples (Golden Delicious, Red Pippin, or Granny Smith)**
* ⅓ **cup sugar**
* ½ **cup ground almonds**
* ⅓ **cup cream**
* **Few drops of almond and/or vanilla extract**

Roll the puff pastry to a thickness of ¼ inch and in a rectangular shape about 10 by 18 inches. Trim the edges, then cut a strip 1 inch wide from each edge. Place the remaining rectangle on a baking sheet and brush an inch of the rectangle's border with water. Place the strips on top of this border, keeping the outer edges even and overlapping the corners. Trim off any extra dough. Chill this pastry case well.

Peel, core, and halve the apples, then place them cut side down on a work surface and cut them into thin slices. Take the pastry case out of the refrigerator and arrange the apple slices in it in a single overlapping layer, being careful not to cover the border.

Sprinkle the tart with 1 tablespoon of sugar and bake it in a preheated 400°F oven until the sides have risen, about 15 minutes.

While the tart is baking, mix the remaining sugar with the ground almonds, cream, and flavoring. Remove the tart briefly from the oven, spread it with the almond mixture, and return it to the oven to finish baking, about 20 minutes more, until it is brown and crisp. You may serve it warm or at room temperature.

FOUR MENUS TO PLEASE HUNTING FRIENDS

IV

Crème de Champignons des Bois
Wild Mushroom Soup

Faisan en Chartreuse
Roast Pheasant with Cabbage

Fromage
Cheese (Livarot)

Douillons
Apples Baked in Puff Pastry

Wine: A Nuits-Saint-Georges with the
whole menu

Crème de Champignons des Bois

Wild Mushroom Soup

Serves 4 to 6

Fresh mushrooms from the Norman forest are difficult to obtain in America. However, this soup has much the same rich flavor and delicious perfume as if it were made with fresh wild mushrooms.

> 1½ ounces dried Boletus mushrooms (*cèpes* or
>   *porcini*) or morels
> 3½ cups beef stock
> 3 tablespoons butter
> 3 tablespoons finely chopped shallots
> 1 pound firm white mushrooms, cleaned and finely
>   chopped
> ¼ teaspoon dried thyme
> Salt and freshly ground pepper
> 1 tablespoon flour
> ½ cup port
> 1 cup heavy cream
> Minced parsley (for garnish)

Soak the dried mushrooms in 1½ cups of the stock for 30 minutes. Drain them, reserving the stock. Rinse the mushrooms in cold water to rid them of any sand that may still be clinging to them, and strain the stock through a sieve lined with a coffee filter or a paper towel. Dry the mushrooms and chop them coarsely.

Melt the butter in a heavy saucepan and sauté the shallots until they are soft. Add the chopped fresh mushrooms, thyme, salt, and pepper, and sauté over moderate heat for 10 minutes, or until most of the mushroom liquid has evaporated. Sprinkle the mixture with flour and continue cooking for about 2 minutes. Add the remaining stock, the wild mushrooms, and the port. Bring the mixture to a boil, reduce the heat, and simmer it, covered, for 20 minutes, stirring occasionally. Add the cream and simmer the soup for 10 minutes more, stirring occasionally. Correct the seasoning. Serve the soup in small bowls and garnish it with minced parsley.

Faisan en Chartreuse

Roast Pheasant with Cabbage

Serves 6

En chartreuse usually means that a dish is served with cabbage. Years ago it meant that it was served with an elaborate vegetable garnish. This way of presenting food probably takes its name from the Carthusian monks, who were strict vegetarians.

> 2 pheasants, about 3½ to 4 pounds each, or
>   guinea hens
> 1 large cabbage (Savoy, if possible), quartered
> 1 pound slab bacon, diced and blanched
> 1 large onion, chopped
> 2 carrots, sliced
> * Bouquet garni
> 1 clove garlic, crushed
> * 1 quart chicken stock
> 1 large garlic sausage or kielbasa, cut into pieces
>   and blanched
> 6 small link sausages browned and drained

Truss the pheasants and roast them in a preheated 425°F oven for 45 minutes, turning them every 10 minutes to insure even browning.

While they are cooking, blanch the cabbage in boiling water for 5 minutes, then drain it. Brown the diced, blanched bacon in a large, heavy casserole with a lid. Add the onion and carrots to the casserole and cook 2 minutes; then add the blanched cabbage quarters.

When the pheasants are roasted, cut them into serving pieces and arrange them on top of the cabbage in the casserole. Add the bouquet garni, garlic, and any cooking juices from the roasted birds, and moisten the dish halfway up with chicken stock. Cover the casserole and bake it at 350°F for 1½ hours. Add the blanched garlic sausage after 45 minutes and the browned sausage links for the final 15 minutes of cooking.

To serve, arrange the pheasant and sausage pieces on top of the cabbage on a large platter and moisten with the cooking juices, or, for an informal meal, serve directly from the casserole.

Douillons

Apples Baked in Puff Pastry

Serves 4

   * ¾ pound puff pastry or demi-puff pastry
    4 medium Granny Smith apples, peeled and cored
    Cinnamon
    Sugar
    1 egg yolk beaten with 1 teaspoon water
    1 cup heavy cream, lightly whipped
    ½ cup apricot jam, warmed

Roll out the pastry into four circles, each of them 12 inches in diameter. Place an apple in the center of each circle. Sprinkle them with cinnamon and sugar. Brush the edge of each circle with the egg-yolk mixture, then fold up the pastry to enclose the apple, press firmly to seal, and invert the apples onto a buttered baking sheet. If you wish, decorate them with pastry trimmings cut into leaf shapes. Glaze the pastry with the remaining egg-yolk mixture and bake the apples in a preheated 375°F oven until the pastry is brown and the apples are tender, about 35 minutes.

To serve, turn the apples fold side up, cut the tops off the pastry, and fill each apple core with whipped cream and warm apricot jam.

THREE FESTIVE AUTUMN MENUS

The first moments of autumn melancholy at La Coquetterie are quickly dispelled by the arrival of friends who drive out from Paris for a few festive days of treasure hunting at the Rouen Antique Fair, which begins around the fifteenth of October

Rouen is the center of the Norman antique trade. The narrow streets to the north of the cathedral, closed to automobile traffic, are crowded with antiquarians' shops, and it is not unusual to discover in them a longed-for armoire or a lovely piece of faïence. These, then, are the menus I use to celebrate successful hunting of a different sort.

I: LUNCH

Timbale de Carottes
Molded Carrot Pudding

Jambonettes de Volaille
Boned Stuffed Chicken Breasts

Salade de Roquette
Wild Lettuce Salad

Mousse Glacée au Calvados
Cold Calvados Mousse

Wine: A Chinon with the whole menu

Timbale de Carottes

Molded Carrot Pudding

Serves 4

For the pudding:
1½ pounds carrots, peeled
2 tablespoons butter
½ teaspoon salt
6 eggs
¼ cup heavy cream
1 to 1½ tablespoons lemon juice
Salt and freshly ground pepper
Nutmeg
3 slices bacon, cooked and crumbled
Parsley (for garnish)

For the hollandaise sauce:
2 egg yolks
2 tablespoons lemon juice
Salt and freshly ground pepper
1 stick butter, melted

To make the pudding:
Cut 2 carrots into thin slices and reserve them for decoration. Cut the rest of the carrots into large pieces and place them in a saucepan with the butter, salt, and enough water to cover. Cook until they are tender, about 20 minutes, then drain and cool them.

Butter and flour a 5-cup charlotte mold or ring mold. In a food processor or food mill, purée the cooked, cooled carrots and beat in the eggs, cream, and lemon juice. Season with salt, pepper, and nutmeg to taste. Layer one-fourth of the carrot mixture, followed by one-third of the bacon, in the mold; repeat twice, ending with the carrot mixture. Bake the pudding in a water bath in a preheated 375°F oven for about 30 minutes, or until a knife inserted into the center comes out clean.

Cook the reserved carrot slices in boiling, salted water until they are tender, then drain them.

To make the hollandaise sauce:
In a blender or food processor, combine the egg yolks, lemon juice, and a pinch each of salt and pepper. Blend for about 1 minute, then pour in the hot melted butter in a thin stream while the machine is running. Correct the seasoning if necessary, and serve the sauce immediately.

To serve:
Unmold the pudding onto a serving plate. Make an attractive garnish with the carrot slices and parsley, and serve with the hollandaise sauce.

Jambonettes de Volaille

Boned Stuffed Chicken Breasts

Serves 4

A large chicken, 3 to 3½ pounds, with wing tips and neck removed and reserved

For the stock:
Bones, wing tips, and neck from chicken
1 carrot, diced
1 onion, diced
1 stalk celery, diced
1 to 2 tablespoons butter
* Bouquet garni
1 chicken bouillon cube

½ pound green beans, washed and trimmed
½ pound carrots, peeled
2 tablespoons heavy cream
Salt and freshly ground pepper
1 tablespoon oil
1 tablespoon butter

For the sauce:
5 shallots, minced
½ cup dry white wine

To bone the chicken:
Using a sharp knife, cut down the breastbone and against the ribcage to free the breast. Remove the wings, thighs, and drumsticks, cutting through the thigh joints. With your fingers, gently loosen the skin from the thigh and drumstick pieces, then pull the meat out of the skin. Save the skin. Remove the dark meat from the bones and put it in a food processor. Leave the breast meat attached to its skin. You will have two pieces.

To make the stock:
Cut the chicken carcass into several pieces. In a large saucepan, brown all the bones, the wing tips and neck, and the diced vegetables in the butter, then cover them with water. Add the bouquet garni and the bouillon cube and cook over moderate heat, skimming as necessary, until the stock is reduced by one-half. Strain and degrease the liquid.

To assemble the dish:
Slice the beans lengthwise and cut the carrots into julienne strips of about the same size. Blanch the beans and carrots separately until they are almost tender, then refresh them in cold water.

Purée the dark chicken meat in the food processor and add enough cream to give it a smooth, light texture. Season it with salt and pepper. If you wish, poach a small amount of this mousseline mixture and check its consistency and seasoning.

Spread a layer of the mousseline over each breast of chicken; place a layer of carrots and beans on top, then cover them with the rest of the mousseline mixture. Enclose the breasts in the skin you saved from the dark meat and tie them with string to form neat packages.

Brown the breast packages in a heavy skillet in the oil and butter and finish them in a preheated 350°F oven, 15 to 20 minutes.

To make the sauce:
Remove the breasts from the skillet, pour off the fat, and lightly brown the shallots in the same pan. Deglaze the pan with the white wine and reduce the liquid by three-quarters. Add the strained, degreased stock and reduce by three-quarters again. Purée the sauce in a food processor or blender.

To serve:
Slice the breasts crosswise, place them on a serving platter, and surround them with the sauce.

Salade de Roquette

Wild Lettuce Salad

Serves 4

1 pound rocket, or a sharp-flavored lettuce such as
    chicory or curly endive, or a mixture of several
    varieties
6 to 7 tablespoons olive oil
1 teaspoon Dijon mustard
2 tablespoons red wine vinegar
1 small clove garlic, crushed (optional)
Salt and freshly ground pepper

Wash and pick over the rocket or lettuce carefully. Use only the best leaves. Mix the remaining ingredients together in a covered jar and shake well to make a vinaigrette. Dress and toss the salad just before serving.

Mousse Glacée au Calvados

Cold Calvados Mousse

Serves 4

1½ pounds tart apples, peeled, cored, and
    quartered
3 tablespoons brown sugar
2 tablespoons apricot jam
6 egg yolks
⅓ cup sugar
⅓ cup Calvados
1½ envelopes gelatin
2 tablespoons lemon juice
2 tablespoons cold water
½ cup heavy cream, whipped
Grated zest of 1 lemon
½ apple, sliced (for garnish)
½ cup apricot jam (for glaze)
2 tablespoons lemon juice (for glaze)

In a large saucepan, cook the apples over moderate heat with the brown sugar and the apricot jam until they are soft, stirring occasionally to prevent sticking. Mash the cooked apples with a fork or purée them in a food processor or blender. Cool them.

In a bowl, beat the egg yolks and sugar until they are thick and light in color. Add the Calvados, place the mixture in the top of a double boiler, and whisk over hot water. The mixture will be frothy at first, but will gradually thicken.

Soften the gelatin in the lemon juice and cold water. Add it to the thickened egg-yolk mixture and continue to whisk, checking to be sure the gelatin has thoroughly dissolved. Remove the mixture from the heat, place it in a large bowl, and chill until it is partially set, about 15 minutes.

When the egg-yolk mixture is fairly firm, fold in the applesauce, whipped cream, and grated lemon zest. Taste it and add more Calvados if you wish. Pour the mousse into an oiled 6-cup mold that you have rinsed with cold water and chill it until it is set, about 3 hours.

To make the garnish, poach the apple slices in water until they are just tender. Cool them in their liquid, then drain them. Strain the apricot jam and melt it in a saucepan with the lemon juice. Let it stand to cool.

To serve the mousse, unmold it onto a serving platter and decorate it with the drained apple slices. Pour on the cooled apricot jam glaze and serve.

THREE FESTIVE AUTUMN MENUS

Soufflé aux Fruits de Mer
Seafood Soufflé

Fricandeau de Veau
Veal Pot Roast

Purée de Laitue
Lettuce Purée

Turban d'Agen
Molded French Rice Pudding with Prunes

Wine: A Chablis with the soufflé,
then a Côte Rôtie

Soufflé aux Fruits de Mer

Seafood Soufflé

Serves 6

2 tablespoons grated Parmesan cheese
6 large sea scallops, cleaned and quartered
12 crayfish or large shrimp, or 1 lobster tail cut in
      rounds
½ pound tiny shrimp, peeled
Juice of 1 lemon
3 tablespoons butter
2 tablespoons flour
¾ cup milk
Salt and freshly ground pepper
Nutmeg
4 egg yolks
1 cup grated Swiss cheese
4 egg whites

Butter a 2-quart oval baking dish or soufflé mold and dust it with
Parmesan cheese.

In a saucepan or skillet, cook all the seafood in the lemon juice
very gently for 4 to 5 minutes. Strain and reserve the cooking
juices.

Melt the butter in a saucepan. Add the flour and cook for several
minutes, but do not brown. Add the reserved seafood cooking
juices and the milk and cook, stirring, until the mixture is very
thick. Season it to taste with salt, pepper, and nutmeg.

Transfer mixture into a large bowl and add the egg yolks, one at
a time. Beat well after each addition, then add half the grated
Swiss cheese. In a separate bowl, beat the egg whites until they are
stiff. Fold them gently into the soufflé mixture.

Spread half the soufflé mixture in the buttered mold. Arrange
the seafood on top and cover it with the remaining soufflé mix-

ture. Top with the rest of the Swiss cheese. Place it in a preheated 425°F oven, reduce the temperature to 400°F, and cook until the soufflé is well puffed and browned on top, about 25 minutes. Serve at once.

Fricandeau de Veau

Veal Pot Roast

Serves 6

3 pounds top round of veal, cut about 2½ or 3
    inches thick
Larding fat and a larding needle, or have the veal
    larded by your butcher
Ham (optional)
3 carrots, diced
2 onions, diced
Oil
About 3 cups beef or veal stock
* Bouquet garni
1 tablespoon arrowroot or cornstarch
½ cup white wine or vermouth

Lard the veal in about five places. If you have any ham, you may alternate it with the fat to form a more interesting design.

In a heavy casserole with a lid, brown the carrots and onions in a little oil until they are golden. Place the roast on top of the bed of vegetables and add stock until it reaches halfway up the roast; add the bouquet garni. Place the casserole in a preheated 350°F oven and braise, covered, about 1½ hours, until the meat is very tender. Baste the veal every 20 minutes with the remaining stock and the accumulated pan juices.

When the roast is done, remove it and keep it warm. Strain the liquid in which it cooked and reduce it to approximately 1½ cups.

To thicken it, mix the arrowroot or cornstarch and wine in a separate bowl, add them to the sauce, and boil, stirring constantly, until the sauce is slightly syrupy, about 2 to 3 minutes. Serve the sauce separately.

Purée de Laitue

Lettuce Purée

Serves 6

4 or 5 heads romaine lettuce, washed, separated,
    and with stems removed
4 tablespoons butter, at room temperature
1 cup cream
Salt and freshly ground pepper

Cook the lettuce for 7 minutes in a large quantity of boiling water, then refresh it in cold water. Squeeze it dry by handfuls. Purée it in a food processor or blender. Add the butter and cream and season to taste with salt and pepper. Heat the purée gently. (You may make it ahead and reheat it.)

Turban d'Agen

Molded French Rice Pudding with Prunes

Serves 6 to 8

The prunes of Agen are thought to be the best in France. However, in the summer I sometimes make this dessert with strawberries in raspberry sauce (*Fraises Cardinal*, p. 39).

6 tablespoons Italian Arborio rice
2 cups milk
Pinch of salt
½ cup sugar
1 teaspoon vanilla extract
2 teaspoons gelatin softened in 2 tablespoons cold
    water
1 cup pitted prunes
¾ cup red currant jelly
¼ cup kirsch
⅓ cup heavy cream

Drop the rice into 2 cups rapidly boiling water and boil, stirring occasionally, for 6 minutes. Bring the milk to a boil with a pinch of salt in a large saucepan. Drain the rice and add it to the milk; cook gently over low heat for about 30 minutes. After 15 minutes add the sugar, vanilla, and softened gelatin and stir well. Continue cooking for 15 minutes more, then remove it from the heat and let it cool.

Stew the prunes in 3 cups water or tea for about 15 minutes, then drain. Warm the currant jelly to soften it, and mix it with the kirsch. Soak the prunes in this sauce for 1 hour.

Whip the heavy cream in a separate bowl and stir it into the cooled rice mixture. Put it into an oiled 3- to 4-cup ring mold and chill.

To serve, unmold the pudding onto a serving platter, fill its center with the prunes, and pour any remaining sauce around the bottom of the rice.

THREE FESTIVE AUTUMN MENUS

Terrine de Coquilles Saint-Jacques, Sauce Pernod
Scallop Terrine with Pernod Mayonnaise

Magrets de Canard Saint-Wandrille
Breast of Duck with Honey and Vinegar

Riz Sauvage
Wild Rice

Salade de Saison
Mixed Green Salad

Soufflé à l'Abricot
Cold Apricot Soufflé

Wine: A Chablis with the first course,
then a Pomerol

Terrine de Coquilles Saint-Jacques, Sauce Pernod

Scallop Terrine with Pernod Mayonnaise

Serves 6

For the terrine:
¾ pound fresh cod, red snapper, or pike, skinned
    and boned
1½ pounds scallops
2 small egg whites
1 cup heavy cream
Salt and freshly ground pepper
Nutmeg
Paprika

For the sauce:
1 egg
2 egg yolks
About ¼ teaspoon each salt and freshly ground
    pepper
2 tablespoons vinegar
2 tablespoons Dijon mustard
¾ cup olive oil
1 cup vegetable oil
2 tablespoons Pernod

To make the terrine:
Cut the fish into pieces and place it and half the scallops in a food
processor; purée until smooth. Add the egg whites and cream, and
season to taste with salt, pepper, nutmeg, and paprika. Process the
mixture until it is well mixed. Cook a spoonful in simmering salted
water to test it for seasoning; correct the seasoning if necessary.
Chill the mousseline mixture.

Heavily butter a 1-quart terrine and line its bottom with buttered wax paper or parchment. Spread half the fish-and-scallop mousseline in the terrine, then place the remaining, whole scallops, patted dry, on top. Cover them with the remaining mousseline to fill the terrine. If the mold is short and deep, make three layers of mousseline and two layers of whole scallops.

Cover the terrine with buttered foil and place it in a roasting pan. Add water until it comes about one-third up the sides of the terrine; gently boil for 5 to 7 minutes on top of the stove to cook the bottom. Then bake the terrine in the water bath in a preheated 375°F oven until a knife inserted in the center comes out clean, about 25 minutes. Serve the terrine lukewarm with the Pernod mayonnaise.

To make the sauce:
Place the egg and egg yolks, salt, pepper, 1 tablespoon of vinegar, and the mustard in a food processor or blender. Mix until the sauce is smooth and the salt is dissolved. With the machine running, add the oils in a thin stream, until the mayonnaise is very thick and all the oil is incorporated. Mix in the Pernod and the remaining vinegar to taste. Taste the sauce and season it with more salt and pepper if you wish. This recipe makes about 2 cups.

Magrets de Canard Saint-Wandrille

Breast of Duck with Honey and Vinegar

Serves 6

I have named this recipe for the Benedictine abbey, a few kilometers from La Coquetterie, where we buy our honey. Its founder, the handsome Count Wandrille, decided on his wedding day to dedicate his life to the search for God. He founded the monastery in 649.

> **6 boneless duck breasts, about 8 ounces each**
> **Salt and freshly ground pepper**
> **⅓ cup cider vinegar**
> **2 tablespoons honey**
> *** 2 cups duck stock or rich brown chicken stock**
> **6 tablespoons butter**
> **4 apples**
> **Lemon juice**
> **1½ cups sugar**
> **About ⅓ cup tap water**
> **¾ cup ice water**

Season the duck breasts with salt and pepper. In a heavy skillet, brown the breasts over medium-high heat, starting with the skin side down to render the fat. The meat should be cooked rare, 3 to 4 minutes on each side. Remove the duck to a heated plate and cover it with foil to keep it warm.

Pour the fat out of the skillet and deglaze the pan with the vinegar. Add the honey and stock, stir, and reduce the liquid to about 1 cup. Whisk the butter into the sauce a tablespoon at a time.

Peel, core, and quarter the apples. Trim the quarters into football shapes and rub them with lemon juice.

In a saucepan, combine the sugar with enough tap water to moisten it. Cook over low heat until it reaches a deep golden color. Quickly add the ice water, be careful to stand back from the saucepan, as it will spatter. Add the apples and cook them in this caramel until they are tender.

To serve, arrange the duck breasts on a heated serving platter, pour the sauce over them, and surround them with the caramelized apples.

Note:
In France it is possible to buy just the breast of the duck. If you cannot do so, cut up a whole duck and freeze the legs and thighs.

You can use them later in another dish, such as *Compote de Canard* (page 119).

To cut up a duck, remove the legs and thighs and cut off the wings. Cut down the length of the breastbone on either side of the ridge. Lift off each breast in one piece, separating it from the ribcage.

Riz Sauvage

Wild Rice

Serves 6

1 cup wild rice
4 cups water
Salt

In a sieve, rinse the wild rice under running cold water for several minutes. Drain it well. Place it in a heavy saucepan with the water. Bring it to a boil, reduce the heat, and simmer, covered, for 40 minutes, or until it reaches the desired degree of fluffiness. Uncover, stir with a fork, and simmer for an additional 5 minutes. Drain the rice if necessary and add salt to taste. The rice will have tripled in volume.

Soufflé à l'Abricot

Cold Apricot Soufflé

Serves 8

1 pound dried apricots
⅔ cup orange juice
2 tablespoons Amaretto, or kirsch mixed with
    ¼ teaspoon almond extract
2 envelopes gelatin
2 tablespoons lemon juice
6 eggs
4 egg yolks
⅔ cup sugar
1 cup heavy cream, whipped
3 ounces dried macaroons, crushed

First prepare a soufflé dish that is 7 or 8 inches in diameter. Make a foil or wax-paper collar 3 inches high and long enough to go around the top of the dish. Oil it and secure it in place with string or tape.

In a saucepan, cook the apricots in the orange juice and Amaretto (or the kirsch and almond extract) until they are very tender, about 15 minutes. Drain them, reserving the cooking juices, and purée them in a blender or food processor. You should have about 1⅔ cups of purée. Allow it to cool.

Soften the gelatin in the cooled reserved liquid and lemon juice, then dissolve it over hot water. In a large bowl placed over hot water, beat the eggs and egg yolks with the sugar, by hand or with an electric mixer, until they are thick, foamy, and much lighter in color. Add the dissolved gelatin to the warm egg mixture, stir, and fold in the apricot purée. Chill until the mixture begins to stiffen. Beat the cream in a bowl. When the apricot mixture is cold and beginning to set, fold in the cream. Add additional almond liqueur if you wish.

Pour half the soufflé mixture into the prepared dish; add a layer of crushed macaroons, then the rest of the soufflé mixture. Decorate the top with a band of macaroon crumbs around the edge. Chill the soufflé for at least 3 hours. Remove the foil collar before serving.

TWO DINNERS BY THE FIRE

I

Mouclade
Curried Mussel Stew

Côte de Boeuf à l'Os
Roasted Beef Chop

Pommes de Terre Marie Harel
Stuffed Baked Potatoes with Camembert

Salade de Saison
Mixed Green Salad

Glace Bénédictine
Benedictine Ice Cream

Tuiles aux Amandes
Almond Tile Cookies

Wine: A Muscadet with the *Mouclade,*
then a Châteauneuf-du-Pape

Norman families take the chill off autumn nights by gathering around the fireplace to roast chestnuts and drink cider. This is a pastime as old as time itself. A table laid by the fire is always a welcome sight when cold winds blow. These are two warm and comforting dinners to share *à deux* or when you are relaxing with friends.

Mouclade

Curried Mussel Stew

Serves 4

1½ quarts mussels
1 small onion, minced
1 clove garlic, crushed
* Bouquet garni
1 cup dry white wine
2 tablespoons butter
1 tablespoon flour
2 teaspoons curry powder
⅓ cup heavy cream
Lemon juice
Salt and freshly ground pepper

Scrub the mussels well with a stiff brush and scrape them with a paring knife, if necessary, to remove any barnacles. Rinse the scrubbed mussels in several changes of water to remove as much sand as possible from their interior. Discard any mussels that are not tightly closed.

Place the mussels in a large, heavy Dutch oven with half the minced onion, the garlic, the bouquet garni, and the wine. Cover and steam them over high heat, shaking the pan occasionally, until the mussels have opened, about 5 or 6 minutes. Discard any that are still unopened.

Transfer the remaining mussels to a bowl. Strain the cooking liquid into a saucepan through a sieve lined with a double thickness of rinsed cheesecloth, and reduce it over high heat to 1½ cups. Shell the mussels, remove and discard their black rims, and reserve them, covered.

In a large saucepan, sauté the remaining minced onion in the butter over moderate heat until it has softened. Stir in the flour and cook the roux over low heat, stirring, for 2 minutes. Add the curry powder and cook the mixture, stirring, for 1 minute. Remove the pan from the heat, pour in the hot mussel cooking liquid, and whisk it vigorously until the mixture is thick and smooth.

Simmer the sauce for 5 minutes, then stir in the cream and season with lemon juice, salt, and pepper to taste. Add the reserved mussels and heat them, stirring, for a few seconds, until they are hot. Divide the *Mouclade* between heated soup plates and serve immediately.

Côte de Boeuf à l'Os

Roasted Beef Chop

Serves 4

A prime rib of beef, about 2 pounds
1 tablespoon butter
1 tablespoon vegetable oil
Salt and freshly ground pepper

Ask your butcher to cut the first rib from the small end of a roast. It should be about 2¼ inches thick and include the bone and the fat tied around the roast.

Preheat the oven to 500°F. In a heavy skillet, heat the butter and oil until they are very hot and bubbling. Salt and pepper the beef chop and quickly brown it on both sides. Transfer the beef to a rack in a roasting pan and roast it for 25 minutes (for rare meat). Let the beef chop rest for 5 minutes before you slice it. You may decorate the end of the bone with a paper frill.

Pommes de Terre Marie Harel

Stuffed Baked Potatoes with Camembert

Serves 4

This recipe comes from the historic Hôtel de Dieppe in Rouen and is named for the farmer's wife who invented Camembert cheese in the second half of the eighteenth century.

> **4 medium baking potatoes, washed and dried**
> **8 ounces Camembert cheese**
> **2 tablespoons butter**
> **2 tablespoons cream**
> **Freshly ground pepper**
> **Salt (optional)**
> **Melted butter**

Bake the potatoes in a preheated hot oven (425° to 450°F) until they are done, about 40 minutes. Remove the rind from the cheese and cut the Camembert into small pieces. When the potatoes are done, cut a lengthwise slice off the top of each one and scoop out the pulp, taking care not to break the potato skins. Using a food processor or electric mixer, mix the hot potato pulp with the cheese, butter, and cream. Season to taste with pepper; add salt if necessary. Stuff the potato shells with the filling, drizzle them with melted butter, and brown them under the broiler for a few minutes to gratinée them. Serve immediately.

Glace Bénédictine

Benedictine Ice Cream

Makes 1 quart

The formula for Benedictine liqueur is a closely guarded secret. The liqueur was originally distilled by the monks from wild plants that grow on the cliffs overlooking the old fishing port of Fécamp.

> 2 cups milk
> 6 egg yolks
> 1 cup sugar
> ⅓ cup Benedictine
> 1 cup heavy cream, whipped
> 1 egg white (optional)

In a heavy saucepan, bring the milk to a boil. Remove it from the heat. Beat the egg yolks and sugar in a bowl until they are thick and lighter in color. Add the milk slowly, whisking constantly. Return the mixture to the saucepan and cook over medium heat, stirring constantly, until it is slightly thickened and coats the back of a spoon. Add the Benedictine and chill.

When the mixture is completely cold, fold in the whipped cream and place the mixture in the freezer. When it is almost frozen, remove it and beat it in a food processor or with an electric mixer until it is fluffy. Add the egg white for additional volume, if you wish, and continue beating. Refreeze the ice cream for at least 1 hour, and store it in a freezer container.

Tuiles aux Amandes

Almond Tile Cookies

Makes about 1 pound

The name of these cookies comes from their special shape: roughly a half-cylinder, which is quite similar to the shape of French roof tiles.

½ cup sugar
2 egg whites
½ teaspoon vanilla extract
⅓ cup plus 1 tablespoon flour, sifted
3½ tablespoons melted butter
½ cup slivered almonds

Beat the sugar, egg whites, and vanilla together in a large mixing bowl until they are foamy and the sugar is well dissolved. Fold in the flour, melted butter, and almonds.

Drop the cookie dough by tablespoonfuls onto greased baking sheets and spread it with the back of a spoon into large circles. Bake the cookies in a preheated 375°F oven until they are lightly browned with a darker edge. Remove them from the baking sheets one at a time, and immediately place each one over a rolling pin to harden into the distinctive shape. (You may also use trough-shaped molds for forming these cookies.) Remove them when they are cooled and set. If you can't shape all the cookies before they set, briefly reheat them on the baking sheet in the oven.

TWO DINNERS BY THE FIRE

II

Salade Forestière
Green Salad with Mushrooms, Roquefort, and
Walnuts

Compote de Canard
Duck Stew

Pâtes Fraîches
Fresh Pasta

Île Flottante à l'Orange
Orange-Flavored Floating Island

Wine: A Cahors with the salad and duck,
a Monbazillac with dessert

Salade Forestière

Green Salad with Mushrooms, Roquefort, and Walnuts

Serves 4

1½ tablespoons walnut oil
1½ tablespoons vegetable oil
1 tablespoon white wine vinegar or sherry vinegar
Salt and freshly ground pepper
4 ounces mushrooms, cleaned and with stems
    trimmed
1 small head Boston or butter lettuce, washed and
    dried
3 ounces (about ½ cup) crumbled Roquefort
    cheese, or another soft blue cheese, such as
    Gorgonzola
½ cup walnut meats, coarsely chopped
1 tablespoon chopped chives

To make the vinaigrette dressing, combine the oils, vinegar, and salt and pepper to taste in a jar. Shake the dressing thoroughly to mix. Cut the mushrooms into thin slices, toss them with the dressing, and marinate them at room temperature for about 1 hour.

When you are almost ready to serve the salad, tear the lettuce into bite-sized pieces and place it in a salad bowl. Sprinkle it with the crumbled cheese and chopped walnuts. Pour the marinated mushrooms and vinaigrette dressing over the salad, sprinkle it with chopped chives, and toss well. Serve immediately.

Compote de Canard

Duck Stew

Serves 4

A 3½ pound duck, or 3½ pounds of duck thigh
    and leg pieces
5 ounces bacon, thickly sliced and cut into
    matchsticks
5 or 6 onions
3 shallots
3 to 4 tablespoons flour
¾ cup white or red wine
* 2 cups chicken or duck stock
1 large clove garlic, crushed
2 teaspoons tomato paste
½ pound mushrooms, quartered
2 tablespoons butter
Salt and freshly ground pepper
Lemon juice

Cut the duck into serving-sized pieces. Put the bacon, onions, and shallots in a heavy pan and brown them slowly. Remove them from the pan and put the duck pieces in to brown. When all the duck is evenly browned, pour off the accumulated fat and return the bacon and vegetables to the pan with the duck. Sprinkle with flour, cook for 2 minutes, and add the wine and stock. Bring the liquid to a boil, add the garlic and tomato paste, and cook, covered, over low heat for 35 to 45 minutes, until the duck is done.

Near the end of the cooking time, place the mushrooms in a skillet with the butter, salt, pepper, and lemon juice to taste, and sauté them until browned. Add them to the duck when it is done. Taste the dish and correct the seasoning before serving.

Pâtes Fraîches

Fresh Pasta

Serves 4

I use a food processor to make the pasta dough. It is a quick and easy method.

> **3 cups flour**
> **1 teaspoon salt**
> **2 teaspoons vegetable oil**
> **3 eggs plus enough water to make a scant ¾ cup**

Put 2½ cups of the flour into the food processor with the salt. Process it to mix it well. With the machine running, add the oil and the egg-water mixture and beat the dough for about 1 minute. Add the remaining flour by tablespoonfuls until the dough forms a ball. It should not be sticky. Take it out, wrap it , and chill it for about ½ hour.

Cut the chilled dough into quarters and roll it out very thin (¹⁄₁₆ inch or less) a quarter at a time, keeping the other quarters, wrapped, in the refrigerator. Cut it into narrow strips. It is easy to roll and cut the dough with a pasta machine; just follow the manufacturer's directions. Sprinkle the noodles lightly with the remaining flour and spread them in a single layer to dry for at least 15 minutes.

Cook the fresh pasta in a large quantity of boiling, salted water to which you have added a few tablespoons of oil, for 5 to 8 minutes or just until tender. Drain the noodles and toss them with butter to serve.

Île Flottante à l'Orange

Orange-Flavored Floating Island

Serves 4

Zest of 1 orange, removed in lengthwise sections
   with a vegetable peeler
¼ cup Grand Marnier

For the caramel:
½ cup sugar
¼ cup water

For the meringue:
6 egg whites, at room temperature
¼ teaspoon cream of tartar
Pinch of salt
¾ cup fine granulated sugar

For the crème anglaise:
1¾ cups milk
4 egg yolks
⅓ cup sugar

To prepare the orange zest:
Cut the zest into very thin julienne strips and simmer them in
water for 10 minutes. Drain and refresh them in cold water, then
dry them on paper towels. Macerate the strips in the Grand Marnier for several hours, or overnight. Just before you make the
meringue, drain the strips, reserving the Grand Marnier for the
crème anglaise.

To make the caramel:
Prepare the mold by filling a 2-quart baking dish, soufflé dish, or

charlotte mold with hot water. Let it stand until you are ready to line it with caramel.

Combine the sugar and water in a heavy saucepan. Bring the mixture to a boil, washing down any sugar crystals from the sides of the pan with a brush dipped in cold water until all the sugar is dissolved. Increase the heat to moderately high and cook the syrup, rotating the pan gently, until it is a deep, golden caramel color.

Discard the water from the mold and pour the caramel in, turning the mold in all directions to coat the bottom and sides as evenly as possible. When the caramel has set, turn the mold upside down on wax paper to cool.

To make the meringue:
Using an electric mixer, beat the egg whites in a large bowl until they are foamy. Add the cream of tartar and salt. Gradually increase the mixer speed to fast. When the egg whites form soft peaks, sprinkle in the sugar a tablespoon at a time. After you have added all of the sugar, beat the egg whites for several minutes more, until they form stiff, shining peaks.

Fold in the drained orange zest and fill the caramelized mold with the meringue. Place the mold in a pan of hot water and bake it in the lower third of a preheated 275°F oven for 50 minutes, until the meringue is puffed and lightly browned.

Remove the meringue from the oven and cool it. Cover and refrigerate it if you are not serving the dessert immediately. The meringue will keep for several days in the refrigerator if it is covered with plastic wrap.

To make the crème anglaise:
In a medium-sized, heavy saucepan, bring the milk just to a boil and remove it from the heat. In a separate bowl, beat the egg yolks and sugar until they are light and lemon-colored. Add the scalded milk in a stream, whisking constantly. Return the mixture to the saucepan and cook it over moderately low heat, stirring constantly, until it thickens just enough to coat the back of a spoon.

Remove it from the heat. If necessary, add more Grand Marnier to the marinade, to make ¼ cup. Add this to the sauce, strain it into a metal bowl, and chill over ice. Stir it occasionally. (The sauce may be stored, covered, in the refrigerator for 24 hours.)

When you are ready to serve the *Île Flottante*, unmold the meringue onto a deep, round serving platter and pour some of the *crème anglaise* around it. Serve the remaining sauce separately.

A DINNER FROM
LA BASTIDE DU ROY

Oeufs Tout-Paris
Poached Eggs with Yellow and Pink Hollandaise
Sauce

Aiguillette de Boeuf à la Polignac
Braised Rump Roast

Salade de Saison
Mixed Green Salad

Plateau de Chèvres
Assortment of Goat Cheeses

Soufflé aux Framboises
Raspberry Soufflé

Wine: A Saint-Émilion with the whole menu

Last autumn when my uncle, Prince Louis de Polignac, was visiting Normandy, he reminded me of a wonderful week we spent cooking together several years ago at his eighteenth-century house, La Bastide du Roy, which is located about six miles inland from Antibes on the Côte d'Azur. The weather was superb that October — warm enough to have lunch on the big flagstone terrace overlooking the sea, and cool enough in the evening to enjoy a pot roast that had been slowly simmered. Uncle Louis is devoted to *l'art culinaire* and firmly believes that the best of French cooking traditions should be kept intact. This is one of the dinners we prepared at La Bastide du Roy.

Oeufs Tout-Paris

Poached Eggs with Yellow and Pink Hollandaise Sauce

Serves 6

6 eggs
2 tablespoons white vinegar
Salt
3 egg yolks
Lemon juice
6 ounces (1½ sticks) butter, melted
Freshly ground pepper
1 teaspoon tomato paste
6 rounds bread, 3 to 4 inches in diameter, toasted
Minced parsley (for garnish)
Truffle slices (for garnish)

Poach the eggs with the vinegar in simmering water for about 3½ to 4 minutes. Remove them with a slotted spoon and transfer them to a shallow ovenproof dish containing enough cold water to cover them. Add 2 or 3 tablespoons of salt. Trim the eggs with scissors. If you prepare the eggs ahead of time, place them in the refrigerator until just before serving.

To make the hollandaise sauce, place the egg yolks in a heavy-bottomed saucepan with 2 teaspoons of lemon juice and a pinch of salt. Using a whisk, stir constantly over very low heat until the egg mixture begins to thicken. Do not boil it, or you will have scrambled eggs. Remove the eggs from the heat and very gradually add the melted butter, whisking constantly. The butter should be at about the same temperature as the warmed yolks. Taste the sauce and add more lemon juice and salt and pepper if you wish. If you make the sauce in advance, warm it at the last minute over simmering water.

Heat the dish containing the eggs over low heat. When the water becomes too hot to touch, remove the dish from the heat. Place half the hollandaise sauce in a fresh bowl and add the tomato paste to flavor and color it. Mix well.

Arrange the toast rounds on a warm serving platter. Drain each egg, using a slotted spoon, and place one on each piece of toast. Spoon the two hollandaise sauces over the eggs, alternating yellow and pink, or make each egg half pink and half yellow. Top the pink hollandaise with minced parsley and the yellow hollandaise with truffle slices. Serve hot.

Aiguillette de Boeuf à la Polignac

Braised Rump Roast

Serves 6

A 2½-pound rump roast, pierced with thin strips
    of fat
1 cup dry white wine
¾ cup Cognac
Pinch of allspice
Salt and freshly ground pepper
1 tablespoon butter
2 tablespoons oil
1 veal knuckle or shank
3 large carrots, sliced
3 large onions, sliced
3 shallots, chopped
4 or 5 cloves garlic, crushed
* Large bouquet garni
2 tablespoons tomato paste
* 3 cups chicken stock, or 3 cups water and 2
    chicken bouillon cubes

Marinate the beef for several hours or overnight in the white wine, Cognac, allspice, and salt and pepper to taste. When you are ready to prepare the dish, remove the meat and wipe it dry.

Melt the butter and 1 tablespoon of the oil in a heavy casserole or Dutch oven. Brown the roast on all sides over moderately high heat; remove it. In the same casserole, brown the veal knuckle or shank with the carrots and onions, stirring frequently, until it is golden. Return the roast to the casserole and add the shallots, garlic, marinating liquid, bouquet garni, tomato paste, and stock or water and bouillon cubes. The liquid should come about half-way up the roast. Cover the casserole tightly and simmer for 3½ to 4 hours in a preheated 325°F oven. Baste the meat occasionally.

Remove the roast to a platter and let it stand for 15 minutes before slicing. Strain the cooking juices, reserving the vegetables but discarding the veal and the bouquet garni. Degrease the sauce and reduce it, if necessary, to intensify the flavor. Correct the seasoning.

To serve, make a bed of the vegetables on a deep serving platter. Slice the roast and arrange the slices on top. Moisten the beef with sauce and pass the rest of the sauce at the table. Serve with plenty of hot, crusty French bread.

Soufflé aux Framboises

Raspberry Soufflé

Serves 6

1 pound fresh raspberries or 2 packages frozen
    raspberries
½ cup powdered sugar, or to taste

For the soufflé:
4 egg yolks
6 tablespoons granulated sugar
5 egg whites
Pinch of salt

For the sauce:
1½ teaspoons arrowroot or cornstarch, dissolved in
    a little cold water
2 tablespoons raspberry liqueur or kirsch
Lemon juice

Reserve about 15 berries; purée the rest in a food processor or blender and strain the purée to remove seeds, or pass the berries through a food mill. Sweeten them to taste with powdered sugar, stirring well, until the mixture becomes thick and creamy. Put aside ½ cup of the purée for the soufflé and reserve the rest for the sauce.

To make the soufflé:
Place the egg yolks, 5 tablespoons of granulated sugar, and the ½ cup of raspberry purée in a large, heavy-bottomed saucepan. Beat with an electric mixer for 3 minutes, then place the pan over very low heat and continue beating by hand until the mixture reaches the consistency of mayonnaise, about 10 minutes. Do not let the

mixture get too hot; if necessary, remove the pan from the heat from time to time.

In a large bowl, beat the egg whites with a pinch of salt until they form soft peaks. Add the remaining tablespoon of sugar and continue beating until the eggs form stiff peaks.

Fold a spoonful of the egg whites into the raspberry mixture, then fold all the raspberry mixture gently into the remaining egg whites. Turn the mixture into a buttered soufflé dish to which you have attached a buttered collar, placing the reserved whole berries in a layer in the middle. Bake in a preheated 400°F oven until the soufflé is just set, about 20 minutes. Serve immediately with raspberry sauce.

To make the sauce:
Place the remaining raspberry purée (about 1½ cups) in a small saucepan and bring it to a boil. Stir in the dissolved arrowroot or cornstarch and simmer until thick and clear, 1 or 2 minutes. Add the liqueur or kirsch and lemon juice to taste. Serve warm.

WINTER

Dîner au Robinet
L'Anniversaire de Maman
Two Menus for Entertaining in the Kitchen
Four Favorite Winter Menus

$\mathbf{M}$y mother now lives in Normandy all year long, but years ago La Coquetterie went to sleep for the winter. My family and I stayed in Paris and returned to the country with the swallows in the spring. Our Christmas holidays were always spent at my grandmother's château in Reims with my aunts, uncles, and cousins.

My grandmother, Princess Henri de Polignac, lived in a castle built by her grandmother on a hill overlooking the city. She had a fantastic appetite and spent most of her life on a diet, which never lasted more than three days at a time. She called the hour she spent with her chef each morning "the most important period of the day." Even in a wheelchair at the age of ninety-three she was still giving parties and planning every detail.

Grandmother delighted in arranging her Christmas table. A huge bouquet of white Christmas roses would always be in the center, surrounded by countless tiny silver trays containing small pyramids of candied fruits, chocolates, and cookies. (The pastry shop in Reims made deliveries twice a day.) One of my cousins got a camera for Christmas when he was about ten years old, and year after year he photographed us sitting around the table, our faces flushed almost to violet after we shamelessly indulged in the traditional feast of *foie gras*, oysters on the half-shell, and roast turkey. My mother comes upon one of those old pictures now and then, and we are immediately lost in thoughts of my grandmother's marvelous world.

The great inspiration of my grandmother's grandmother, Madame Louise Pommery, was to make a dry champagne. In 1836, when she created Pommery wine, champagne was chiefly a dessert wine, very popular with women. In 1858, when she was widowed, she became very interested in creating a wine that could be drunk from the beginning to the end of a meal and enjoyed by men as well as women. Her *brut* champagne met with immediate and extraordinary success in England, and in recognition of the patronage of her faithful English clients, the widow Pommery built a vast castle in the English Gothic style of the sixteenth century. It sits on a hill outside of Reims, on top of a subterranean empire of vaults one hundred feet deep and ten miles long that in my grandmother's day sheltered some 12 million bottles of champagne. The caves were chalk quarries in Gallo-Roman times. As we never saw wine making in Normandy, my sister, brother, and I loved to explore the meandering passages and gigantic caverns of the cellars at Reims, watching the mysterious work of blue-smocked men who were accustomed to the quietness of caves.

In keeping with her grandmother's passion, my grandmother had the wonderful idea of the *"dejeuner au Robinet,"* where, as if by magic, a crystal faucet at each guest's place poured forth an endless supply of champagne. In reality a barrel filled with champagne was hidden in another room, and each guest could fill his glass with champagne by turning the tap. This delighted my grandmother's clients, and so intrigued my sister and me that she finally gave us a dinner *au Robinet* in the hope, she said, that we would attract good husbands.

DÎNER AU ROBINET

Soufflés Suisses
Individual Cheese Soufflés with Cream

Jambon en Croute, Sauce Madère
Ham in Pastry with Madeira Sauce

Épinards en Branche
Buttered Spinach

Salade de Saison
Mixed Green Salad

Bombe Surprise
Ice Cream Surprise

Wine: An Avize Blanc de Blancs with the *Soufflés Suisses*,
a Champagne rosé with the ham, and
a Champagne brut with the *Bombe Surprise*

Soufflés Suisses

Individual Cheese Soufflés with Cream

Serves 6

2½ tablespoons butter
3 tablespoons flour
1 cup milk
½ chicken bouillon cube, crumbled
2 or 3 slices onion
5 peppercorns
½ bay leaf
4 egg yolks
5 egg whites
Salt
¾ cup grated Swiss cheese
2 cups cream
Freshly ground pepper
* Bouquet garni
Nutmeg
¼ cup grated Swiss or Parmesan cheese

Melt the butter in a heavy saucepan, add the flour, and cook for 1 or 2 minutes until bubbly. In a separate saucepan, bring the milk to a boil with the crumbled chicken bouillon cube, onion slices, peppercorns, and bay leaf. Strain the milk into the butter-and-flour mixture and bring it to a boil, stirring constantly. Continue cooking for several minutes until the mixture has thickened and is smooth. Remove it from the heat and transfer it into a large bowl. Stir in the egg yolks one at a time, mixing well.

In a separate bowl, beat the egg whites with a pinch of salt to form stiff peaks, then fold them gently into the soufflé base along with the grated Swiss cheese. Taste the mixture and correct the seasoning.

Fill 6 well-greased 1-cup soufflé molds or custard cups with the soufflé mixture. Place the molds in a water bath and bake them in a preheated 375°F oven until they are puffed and browned, about 15 minutes. If you make them ahead, reheat them in a water bath before proceeding to the next step.

While the soufflés are cooking, cook the cream in a saucepan with salt and pepper to taste, the bouquet garni, and a little nutmeg until it is slightly reduced. Unmold the soufflés and place them in an ovenproof serving dish. Cover them with the hot cream, sprinkle with the remaining ¼ cup of cheese, and bake them for 10 to 12 minutes in a preheated 350°F oven, until the cheese has melted and the soufflés have absorbed some of the cream. Serve immediately.

Jambon en Croute, Sauce Madère

Ham in Pastry with Madeira Sauce

Serves 6 to 8

For the pastry:
8 ounces (2 sticks) cold butter, or 4 ounces butter
    and 4 ounces margarine
3½ cups flour
½ teaspoon salt
2 eggs
About ½ cup ice water

A 3- to 4-pound Virginia ham, cooked, or a 2½-
    to 3-pound boned canned ham
1 egg beaten with 1 teaspoon water

For the sauce:
1 tablespoon butter
1 tablespoon oil
2 shallots, diced
2 small carrots, diced
2 onions, diced
Flour
½ cup white wine
* 2 cups brown or beef stock
1 clove garlic, crushed
* Bouquet garni
3 tablespoons Madeira
Salt and freshly ground pepper
3 or 4 tablespoons butter (optional)

To make the pastry:
Combine the butter, flour, and salt and mix until crumbly. Form a well in the center; in a small bowl, beat together the eggs, ice water, and oil and pour them into the well, drawing the dry ingredients into the center until they are combined and well mixed. Form the dough into a ball, wrap it, and chill it for at least ½ hour. (You may make the dough in a food processor.)

To prepare the ham:
The ham should be trimmed, cooked completely, and chilled before you encase it in pastry. Carve the meat in slices from top to bottom, then reassemble it so it looks as though it were still whole. If it has a bone, keep the shank portion, to protrude through the pastry when the ham is covered. The meat should be somewhat pear-shaped.

Roll out the dough until it is about ⅜-inch thick and large enough to enclose the meat. Place the ham in a shallow baking dish. Wrap the pastry around the meat, tucking it underneath to form a neat package. Seal it with the beaten egg and decorate it, if you wish, with pastry cut in the shape of leaves, stuck on with beaten egg. Glaze the pastry with the remaining beaten egg and bake the ham in a preheated 375°F oven until the pastry is browned and the meat is hot, about 35 minutes.

To make the sauce:

Melt the butter with the oil in a large, heavy-bottomed saucepan. Over medium heat, brown the diced vegetables; sprinkle them with flour and continue cooking for 5 minutes. Moisten them with the wine and stock, bring the liquid to a boil, add the garlic and bouquet garni, and reduce the sauce by half.

Strain the sauce. Add the Madeira, return the sauce to a boil, and remove it from the heat. Just before serving, correct the seasoning, adding salt and pepper to taste. Whisk in additional butter, if you wish, for a richer sauce.

To serve:

Place the meat on a warm serving platter. Serve the sauce separately, in a sauceboat.

Épinards en Branche

Buttered Spinach

Serves 6

**3 pounds fresh spinach, well washed and with stems
    removed
4 tablespoons butter
Salt and freshly ground pepper
Nutmeg**

In a large skillet, cook the spinach over medium heat in the water clinging to the leaves. There will be too much spinach for the pan at first, but it will wilt down. Turn it carefully to expose all leaves to the cooking surface, gradually adding the rest of the spinach. When all of the leaves are wilted, add the butter and season to taste with salt, pepper, and nutmeg.

Bombe Surprise

Ice Cream Surprise

Makes 1 quart

1 cup seedless white grapes
½ cup kirsch or plum brandy
6 egg whites
Pinch of salt or cream of tartar
1 cup sugar
About 1 tablespoon water
1 teaspoon vanilla extract
1 cup heavy cream, whipped
1 small jar (6 to 8 ounces) apricot jam
Lemon juice
Kirsch or plum brandy (optional)

Macerate the grapes in the liqueur for 6 to 12 hours in advance.

To make the ice cream, beat the egg whites with salt or cream of tartar until they form soft peaks. Meanwhile, cook the sugar over high heat with a little water. When it reaches the soft-ball stage (about 120°F on a candy thermometer), pour it slowly into the egg whites, beating constantly. Continue beating until the mixture is thick, glossy, and cool. Flavor it with the vanilla, then fold in the whipped cream and the liqueur from the macerated grapes. Freeze in a 1-quart mold.

Alternative method: You may use a quart of ready-made vanilla ice cream. Just soften it slightly, add the liqueur, and press it into a 1-quart mold.

When the ice cream is frozen, scoop out its center, mix it with the grapes, and refill the cavity with the mixture. Refreeze.

To serve, unmold the bombe. Heat the jam, thinned with a little lemon juice and liqueur if you wish, and serve it hot with the bombe.

L'ANNIVERSAIRE DE MAMAN

Délices de Homard, Sauce Pernod à l'Américaine
Lobster Mousse with Pernod Sauce

Escalopes de Veau aux Noisettes
Veal Scallops with Hazelnut Sauce

Endives à l'Orange
Braised Endives with Orange

Salade de Saison
Mixed Green Salad

Chocolat Saint-Émilion
Chocolate Macaroon Cake

Wine: A Montrachet with the lobster and a
Saint-Emilion with the rest of the menu

Family anniversaries are very special in France, and it has become a tradition in our family for my mother to come to Paris to celebrate her birthday. After weeks of rain and winter mist in Normandy, she looks forward to the gaiety of the occasion, for our gatherings *en famille* are usually a good deal of fun.

I enjoy planning a dinner that will delight my mother. She has great respect for the pleasures of the table, even though she regards cooking as a mysterious craft for which she has no special talent.

Délices de Homard, Sauce Pernod à l'Américaine

Lobster Mousse with Pernod Sauce

Serves 6

2 live lobsters, 2 pounds each
2 egg whites
Heavy cream, equal to amount of puréed lobster meat
Salt and freshly ground white pepper
1 tablespoon chopped parsley (for garnish)

For the sauce:
2 tablespoons butter
Lobster shells, cut into pieces
4 tablespoons Cognac
* Bouquet garni
* 4 cups fish stock
9 peppercorns
1 tablespoon tomato paste
Pinch of sugar
Salt
Lobster coral
4 or 5 tablespoons heavy cream
2 tablespoons Pernod
5 tablespoons cold butter, cut into 10 pieces

To prepare the lobsters:
Kill the lobsters by inserting a sharp-pointed knife between their eyes and bearing down. Split them lengthwise. Remove the sacks in the heads and the intestinal tubes, then take out the meat, reserving any juice. Keep the lobster shells, juice, and coral for the sauce.

In a blender or food processor, purée the lobster claw and tail meat in small batches so that it does not become warm. Chill the purée. Place it in a chilled bowl set in a bowl of cracked ice and add the egg whites, beating with a wooden spatula. Then, a little at a time, incorporate the heavy cream. (You may use the food processor to blend the egg whites and cream into the chilled purée.) Season to taste with salt and white pepper.

Butter a small, shallow baking dish and pour in the lobster mousse. Bake it in a water bath in a preheated 400°F oven for about 20 minutes, or until it is just set.

To make the sauce:

In a large saucepan, melt the butter over medium-high heat. Add the lobster shells and sauté them until they turn red. Add the Cognac and ignite it. When the alcohol has burned off, add the bouquet garni, fish stock, peppercorns, tomato paste, a small pinch of sugar, and salt to taste. Cook to reduce the sauce by half. Add the coral and strain. Add the cream and Pernod, bring the sauce to a boil, and remove it from the heat. Whisk in the butter one piece at a time to finish the sauce.

To serve:

Unmold the lobster mousse onto a warm serving platter. Sprinkle it with the chopped parsley. Serve the *sauce Pernod* in a sauceboat.

Escalopes de Veau aux Noisettes

Veal Scallops with Hazelnut Sauce

Serves 6

4 ounces of hazelnuts
4 ounces (1 stick) plus 4 tablespoons butter
12 thin scallops of veal, about 2 ounces each
Flour
Salt and freshly ground pepper
4 tablespoons heavy cream
Worcestershire sauce
Pinch of cayenne

Put the hazelnuts on a baking sheet and toast them in a preheated 350°F oven until they are golden and their skins flake off. To remove the skins, put the nuts into a dry towel and rub them vigorously together.

Grind the hazelnuts in a blender, or grate them in a food processor, using the fine grating disk. Remove the disk and 2 tablespoons of the ground nuts. Using the steel blade, mix the remaining nuts and the stick of butter. Mix them thoroughly, but avoid overheating and melting the butter. Wrap the mixture in a sheet of wax paper and refrigerate it until it is completely cold and hardened. Cut it into medium-sized chunks.

Dredge the scallops in flour seasoned with salt and pepper and shake off the excess. Melt 2 tablespoons of butter in a skillet. Sauté the scallops quickly over high heat, about 2 minutes on each side. Do not crowd the pan. Remove the veal to a heated platter and set it in a warm place. Continue sautéing scallops, adding more butter as necessary, until they are all cooked.

In a saucepan, heat the cream with a dash or two of Worcestershire sauce, salt and pepper, and a tiny pinch of cayenne. Bring it to a boil and reduce it by half. Whisk in the hazelnut butter piece by piece, until it is all incorporated into the sauce. Immediately remove the sauce from the heat and keep it in a warm place.

Serve 2 scallops per person, topped with the sauce and a sprinkling of the remaining ground hazelnuts.

Endives à l'Orange

Braised Endives with Oranges

Serves 6

2½ pounds small Belgian endives
2 oranges
Juice of ½ lemon
6 tablespoons butter
Salt and freshly ground pepper
1 tablespoon powdered sugar

Trim the endives and make conical cuts into the stems to remove them. Wash the endives well, then cook them in boiling, salted water until just tender, about 12 minutes. Drain them and pat them dry on towels. Place them close together in a buttered baking dish. (You may prepare them up to a day ahead of time.)

Remove the zest from the oranges with a vegetable peeler. Cut it into fine strips and drop them into approximately 1 cup of boiling water. When it returns to a boil, remove and drain the zest. Arrange it on and around the endives in the baking pan. Squeeze the juice from the oranges and pour it and the lemon juice over the endives. Dot them with butter and sprinkle them with salt, pepper, and powdered sugar.

Cover the endives with aluminum foil and bake them for 15 minutes in a preheated 375°F oven. Remove the foil and continue baking for 10 to 15 minutes more, until the endives are lightly glazed.

Chocolat Saint-Émilion

Chocolate Macaroon Cake

Serves 6

This is a sinfully rich cake that requires no baking.

> 1¼ cups milk
> 8 ounces (2 sticks) unsalted butter
> ¾ cup sugar
> 2 egg yolks
> 1 pound dark bittersweet chocolate, cut into small
>   pieces
> ½ pound small, dry almond macaroons (Amaretti
>   di Saronno)
> Dark rum

Bring the milk to a boil in a small saucepan, then set it aside to cool. In a bowl, cream the butter with the sugar until it is light and fluffy. In another bowl, add the cooled milk to the egg yolks. Melt the chocolate in the top of a double boiler. Cool it slightly, then stir in the milk-egg mixture and add the butter and sugar. Beat the mixture until it is completely smooth. Brush the macaroons with rum and set them aside.

Oil an 8-inch springform pan and pour a thin layer of the chocolate mixture into it. Arrange a layer of macaroons over the chocolate. Continue filling the pan with layers of chocolate and macaroons until you have used all of the chocolate mixture. Finish with a layer of macaroons.

Refrigerate the cake overnight and unmold it before serving. This cake freezes beautifully.

TWO MENUS FOR
ENTERTAINING IN THE KITCHEN

One of the things that has impressed me the most during my trips through the United States is the charm of American kitchens. A beautiful, hospitable kitchen where the whole family gathers and where one can entertain is quite unusual in France.

Serving dinner in the kitchen takes a little careful thought, for your kitchen must be as neat as your sitting room and everything should seem effortless. The setting should not be spoiled by too many saucepans and dishes.

Dinner in the kitchen is a treatment I reserve for very close friends on informal occasions, such as Sunday evenings. Generally I do not invite more than two couples, and I like to give them an old-fashioned meal that has cooked slowly and that we can eat in a relaxed atmosphere. These are the kind of time-tested menus that the French love.

I

Feuilletés au Chester
Cheddar Cheese Pastries

Cassoulet des Cassoulets
The Best Cassoulet

Salad de Cresson et d'Endive
Watercress and Endive Salad

Tarte à l'Orange Maltaise
Orange Meringue Tart

Wine: A Cahors with the whole menu

Feuilletés au Chester

Cheddar Cheese Pastries

Serves 6

* 1 recipe puff pastry, or demi-puff pastry that has
        been given only 5 turns
  8 ounces English Chester (Cheshire) or Cheddar
        cheese, cut in thin slices
  1 egg yolk beaten with 1 teaspoon water

Roll out the pastry to a ⅛-inch thickness, then cut it into 3-inch
rounds with a crenelated cutter. Turn half of the rounds upside
down onto a cookie sheet that you have sprinkled with water.
Place a slice of cheese on each pastry round, and top them with the
remaining pastry rounds. Brush the tops with the beaten egg yolk
and bake the pastries in a preheated 400°F oven until they are
puffed and golden brown, about 15 minutes. Serve at once.

Variation:
You may make these bite-size to serve with cocktails. Roll grated
cheese into the dough. Sprinkle cheese between all layers during
the first two turns, and give the dough six turns in all. Cut it into
small rounds, brush it with egg, and bake it in a single layer.

Cassoulet des Cassoulets

The Best Cassoulet

Serves 8 to 10

In his book *L'Histoire à Table*, André Castelot teaches us that
Prosper Montagné used to say, "The cassoulet is the God of South

West Cooking. If the cassoulet of Castelnaudary is the Father, then Carcassonne's is the Son and Toulouse's is the Holy Spirit." Of course, none of these three cities is located in Normandy. However, this Holy Trinity reigns over all France, and it would be a pity not to give a recipe for cassoulet in this book. Mine is rather half Carcassonne and half Toulouse, since it contains lamb, pork, and sausage. While it is cooking, a crust appears on top. This crust must be broken and melted in the cassoulet. The more the cassoulet cooks, the better it is, and it is a very old tradition to let the crust appear seven times.

> 2 pounds white navy beans
> 1 pig's foot (if available)
> 1 pound salt pork with streaks of lean
> 1 whole onion, stuck with 3 cloves
> 1 large carrot, quartered
> 3 tablespoons lard
> 3 onions, sliced
> 1 large carrot, sliced
> 3 cloves garlic, minced
> 1 tablespoon flour
> * 1 to 1½ quarts brown stock
> * Bouquet garni
> Pinch of saffron
> 4 tomatoes, peeled, seeded, and chopped
> A 2-pound leg of lamb or lamb shoulder
> ½ cup dry white wine
> 1 clove garlic, halved
> 1 large garlic sausage or kielbasa
> 1 cup soft bread crumbs
> 3 tablespoons minced parsley
> 3 to 4 tablespoons goose fat or butter, melted

Soak the beans overnight in enough cold water to cover them. Bring them to a boil in a large saucepan; let boil 5 minutes and drain them. Cover the beans with fresh water. Add the pig's foot, salt pork, onion, and quartered carrot; simmer until the beans are nearly cooked, approximately 1 hour. Drain them, reserving the liquid. Discard the pig's foot, onion, and carrot. Remove the salt pork and cut it into cubes.

Melt 2 tablespoons of lard in a heavy casserole. Sauté the salt pork, sliced onions and carrot, and minced garlic until they are lightly golden. Sprinkle them with flour and cook for 1 minute, stirring. Add 1 quart of stock and the bouquet garni, saffron, and tomatoes. Boil until the liquid is reduced by half. Remove it from the heat, drain and set aside the vegetables, and reserve the liquid.

Brown the lamb in 1 tablespoon of lard in the casserole. Add the wine and the reduced stock. Simmer for 1 hour; remove from the heat, and set aside the lamb and the liquid.

Rub the bottom and sides of the casserole with garlic. Add a layer of beans. Cut the lamb into thick slices and arrange it on top of the beans. Cover it with more beans and half of the cooking liquid. Cut the sausage in thick slices and arrange it on top of the beans. Cover this with the rest of the beans, and pour on the rest of the liquid from the lamb. If you cannot see the liquid through the top layer of beans, add more stock or a little of the water in which the beans were cooked.

Cover the top layer of beans with a thick layer of bread crumbs and parsley. Place the casserole in a preheated 375°F oven and bake, uncovered, for 1½ to 2 hours. Every time a crisp crust forms, break it with a wooden spoon and stir it down into the beans. Serve the cassoulet very hot from the casserole.

Salade de Cresson et d'Endive

Watercress and Endive Salad

Serves 8

2 bunches watercress
3 medium or 4 small Belgian endives
4 tablespoons olive oil
5 tablespoons vegetable oil
2 to 3 tablespoons lemon juice, or to taste
1 to 2 teaspoons Dijon mustard or ¼ teaspoon dry
    mustard
½ small clove garlic, mashed
Salt and freshly ground pepper

Wash and pick over the watercress, removing any large stems. Separate the leaves of the endive and wash them. Spin the greens dry. In a jar or small bowl, mix together the remaining ingredients to make a vinaigrette; shake or stir them well to combine them.

Toss the watercress with enough vinaigrette to coat the leaves lightly, and divide it among chilled salad plates. Arrange the endives on top, tips pointing outward in a sunburst pattern, with a sprig of watercress in the center of each plate. Drizzle the salad with the remaining vinaigrette.

You may cut the endives into 1-inch pieces and toss them with the watercress for an alternative presentation.

Tarte à l'Orange Maltaise

Orange Meringue Tart

Serves 8

* 1 recipe *pâte sucrée*
   4 tablespoons apricot jam or orange marmalade,
      warmed
   3 large oranges (blood oranges, if possible)
   1 lemon
   1 tablespoon orange liqueur
   1½ cups sugar
   6 tablespoons butter at room temperature (add a
      pinch of salt, if unsalted)
   1 egg
   4 egg yolks
   4 egg whites
   ¼ teaspoon cream of tartar
   1 teaspoon vanilla extract

Roll out the pastry dough until it is ⅛-inch thick and with it line a 10-inch tart pan with a removable bottom. Chill the shell for 1 hour. Line the chilled pastry shell with foil and fill it with rice, then bake it in a preheated 375°F oven for 15 minutes. Remove the rice and foil, paint the shell with the jam or marmalade, and return it to the oven for 10 minutes more. Remove and cool it.

Grate the zest from 2 oranges and 1 lemon. Mix the grated zest of 1 orange with 1 tablespoon of orange liqueur and set it aside for the meringue. Peel the oranges and the lemon and cut the sections away from the membranes. Place the sections in a food processor with 1 cup of sugar and the butter, whole egg and egg yolks, and remaining zests. Process them for about 2 minutes. The mixture will look curdled at first, but will become thicker and homogeneous. Pour it into the cooled tart shell and bake it in a preheated

350°F oven until it is set, about 30 to 35 minutes. Remove it from the oven and cool it.

When the tart has cooled to room temperature, beat the egg whites with the cream of tartar. When they form soft peaks, begin adding the remaining ½ cup of sugar gradually. Add the orange zest soaked in liqueur and the vanilla and continue beating for about 5 minutes, until the meringue is stiff and glossy. Spread it on top of the tart and bake the tart once more, in a 325°F oven, until it is golden brown. Cool it before serving.

TWO MENUS FOR
ENTERTAINING IN THE KITCHEN

II

Ramequins "Vieux Puits"
Flan of Leeks, Endive, and Smoked Haddock

Gigot de Sept Heures
Seven-Hour Leg of Lamb

Carottes et Navets Étuvés au Beurre
Buttered Carrots and Turnips

Salade de Trevise et de Mâche
Red and Green Salad

Tarte Herminia
Upside-Down Apple Tart

Wine: A Gros Plant with the flan, then a Pauillac

Ramequins "Vieux Puits"

Flan of Leeks, Endive, and Smoked Haddock

Serves 6

In the old town of Pont-Audemer, fanciful timbered houses are built over little tributaries of the river Risle. The Auberge le Vieux Puits is a marvelous example of this kind of quaint Norman architecture, and it is where I discovered these *ramequins*.

> 8 ounces smoked haddock (finnan haddie), or
>   smoked cod
> Milk
> 3 or 4 leeks
> 2 or 3 Belgian endives
> 3 or 4 tablespoons butter
> 1½ cups cream or half-and-half
> 3 large eggs
> Cayenne
> Dry mustard
> Nutmeg
> Salt (optional)
> About ¼ cup grated Parmesan cheese

Soak the smoked haddock in enough milk to cover it for at least 1 hour, or up to 24 hours in advance. Rinse, dry, and mince the soaked haddock. Wash the vegetables well, trim them, and cut them into thin slices. You will need about 1½ cups of each vegetable. Gently sauté the vegetables in 3 tablespoons of butter over low heat, about 15 minutes, until they are transparent and wilted. Add more butter if necessary. Cover the pan if they start to brown.

Mix the cream or half-and-half and eggs in a large bowl. Add the fish and vegetables. Season highly with cayenne, dry mustard, and nutmeg, adding salt to taste only if necessary.

Pour the mixture into a buttered, deep ceramic tart mold about 10 inches in diameter, or buttered individual ramekins. Sprinkle it with Parmesan cheese and bake for 35 to 45 minutes in a pre-heated 350°F oven, until the flan is set and a knife inserted in the center comes out clean. Let the flan stand for about 10 minutes before serving.

Gigot de Sept Heures

Seven-Hour Leg of Lamb

Serves 6

This is a very old recipe, still popular in many rural parts of France. It requires time but very little effort. The meat will be tender enough to eat with a spoon.

> **A 5-pound leg of lamb**
> **4 cloves garlic**
> **3 tablespoons butter**
> **3 carrots, sliced**
> **3 medium onions, sliced**
> **1 cup dry white wine**
> **1 cup beef bouillon or *brown stock**
> **1 tablespoon tomato paste**
> **Salt and freshly ground pepper**
> *** Bouquet garni**

Trim as much fat as possible from the lamb. Cut the garlic into lengthwise slivers and insert it into pockets you have cut in the meat. Tie the roast and brown it over medium heat in butter, with the carrots and onions, in a heavy Dutch oven. Add the wine, cook 1 minute, then add the bouillon or stock and tomato paste. Season with salt and pepper to taste and add a large bouquet garni.

Cover the casserole and roast the lamb in a very slow preheated oven, at 250° to 275°F, for 6 to 7 hours. Remove the leg of lamb to a serving platter. Strain the cooking liquid and pour it over the meat.

Carottes et Navets Étuvés au Beurre

Buttered Carrots and Turnips

Serves 6

1 pound carrots, peeled and sliced ¼-inch thick
1½ pounds turnips, peeled, halved, and sliced
    ⅜-inch thick
* 2 cups chicken or veal stock, or water
1 to 2 teaspoons sugar
3 tablespoons butter
Salt and freshly ground pepper
1 tablespoon minced fresh parsley (for garnish)

Place the carrots and turnips in a large saucepan with the stock or water, sugar, butter, and salt and pepper to taste. Cook them, partially covered, over medium heat until they are tender and the liquid has evaporated, about 30 minutes. Correct the seasoning if necessary. Serve the vegetables, sprinkled with parsley, in a warmed serving dish.

Salade de Trevise et de Mâche

Red and Green Salad

Serves 6

3 small heads bitter red lettuce (radicchio)
1 pound lamb's lettuce or young spinach leaves
4 to 5 tablespoons olive oil
4 tablespoons vegetable oil
2 tablespoons vinegar
2 teaspoons Dijon mustard
½ clove garlic, crushed (optional)
1 tablespoon minced chives
1 tablespoon minced parsley
Salt and freshly ground pepper to taste

Wash the lettuce very well to remove all sand, and spin it dry. Chill it until you are ready to serve.

Whisk all the remaining ingredients in a small bowl or shake them together in a covered jar. Taste this vinaigrette to check the seasoning. Toss it with the lettuce just before serving.

Tarte Herminia

Upside-Down Apple Tart

Serves 6

5 or 6 tart apples
Lemon juice
6 to 8 tablespoons butter
4 tablespoons sugar, or to taste
Pinch of cinnamon
* 1 pound puff pastry
* 1 cup *crème fraîche* or whipped cream

Peel and quarter the apples and rub them with lemon juice to prevent discoloration. Heat the butter in a large skillet until foamy. Add the apples and sprinkle them with sugar. Cook until they are lightly browned, stirring occasionally. If they are very tart, add a little more sugar. Arrange the apples in concentric circles in a buttered 9- or 10-inch cake pan, leaving a little space at the edge. Sprinkle with cinnamon.

Roll out the pastry until it is ⅜-inch thick, and cut a circle about 3 inches larger than the diameter of the cake pan. Place this over the apples, tucking it neatly around the edges of the fruit.

Bake the tart in a preheated 375°F oven until it is well browned, about 25 minutes. Cool it for 5 minutes in the pan, then unmold it onto a serving plate. Serve it with *crème fraîche* or lightly whipped cream.

FOUR FAVORITE WINTER MENUS

I

Tarte aux Poireaux
Leek Quiche

Poulet Sauté aux Échalotes
Sautéed Chicken with Shallots

Pommes de Terre à la Sarladaise
Sautéed Potatoes with Truffles

Salade de Saison
Mixed Green Salad

Pommes au Four Frangipane
Baked Apples with Almond Cream

Wine: A Bourgueil with the whole menu

My teenaged children consider themselves very sophisticated. However, when they invite guests to dinner, they like uncomplicated food that everyone can enjoy, presented in a special way. This menu is one of their favorites.

Tarte aux Poireaux

Leek Quiche

Serves 6 to 8

For the pastry:
1 cup flour
Pinch of salt
2 ounces (4 tablespoons) butter
1 egg
Cold water (if necessary)

For the filling:
3 tablespoons butter
1½ pounds leeks
3 egg yolks
⅔ cup heavy cream
Salt and freshly ground pepper
Nutmeg

To make the pastry:
In a food processor or by hand, combine the flour, salt, and butter. Mix until it is crumbly. Add the egg and quickly blend it in. The dough should form a ball. If it is too dry, add a little cold water. Turn the dough onto a smooth work surface and finish mixing it, if necessary. Press it with your hand into a neat, flat oval, then wrap it in wax paper and refrigerate for at least 1 hour.

To make the filling:
Melt the butter in a heavy skillet over low heat. Wash the leeks several times. Trim them, slice them in very thin rounds, and add them to the melted butter. Cover and cook slowly until the leeks are tender, stirring from time to time. Remove them from the heat.

In a bowl, whisk together the egg yolks and cream. Season them to taste with salt, pepper, and nutmeg, and add them to the leeks. Mix well and set aside.

To make the quiche:
Grease an 8- or 9-inch tart pan. Roll out the dough until it is very thin and line the tart pan with it. Pour in the filling and cook the quiche on a baking sheet in the center rack of a preheated 400°F oven, about 25 to 30 minutes. Let it set for a few minutes after removing it from the oven, then serve it hot.

Poulet Sauté aux Échalotes

Sautéed Chicken with Shallots

Serves 8

You may make this dish several hours in advance and reheat it.

> 2 chickens, 3 pounds each
> 4 tablespoons butter
> Salt and freshly ground pepper
> 1½ pounds shallots, peeled and finely chopped
> 1 scant tablespoon flour
> * 1½ cups chicken stock
> Juice of 1 lemon

Cut the chickens into eight pieces each. In a large skillet, gently sauté the pieces in 2 or 3 tablespoons of butter, turning them from time to time, for 15 minutes. You will have to cook them in batches to avoid crowding the pan. Remove them and season them to taste with salt and pepper. Add the shallots to the pan and gently cook them without allowing them to color. Remove them and set them aside with the chicken.

Add the remaining butter to the skillet. Add the flour and cook for 1 minute, then add the chicken stock and bring it to a boil.

Return the shallots and all the chicken pieces to the skillet. Add the lemon juice and cook gently over low heat for 15 minutes. Correct the seasoning, and thin the sauce with a little water if it is too thick. Serve the chicken in a deep dish with the sauce poured over it.

Pommes de Terre à la Sarladaise

Sautéed Potatoes with Truffles

Serves 6

3 pounds potatoes
5 tablespoons butter or 3 tablespoons goose fat
    (optional)
1 teaspoon salt
1 teaspoon freshly ground pepper
1 can of truffles, with their juice
1 tablespoon fresh parsley (for garnish)

Peel the potatoes and cut them into thin slices. Melt the butter or the goose fat in a skillet (you can use 2 tablespoons of each). Add the potatoes and cook over low heat for about 25 minutes, stirring occasionally. Season them with salt and pepper.

When you are ready to serve, cut the truffles into thin slices and add them and their juice. Correct the seasoning if necessary. Place the potatoes on a nice platter with the pan juices and sprinkle them with chopped parsley.

Pommes au Four Frangipane

Baked Apples with Almond Cream

Serves 6

6 medium apples
Lemon juice
1 cup powdered sugar
4 ounces (1 stick) butter
1 cup ground almonds, made from ¾ cup whole
    blanched almonds finely ground with 1
    tablespoon flour
1 egg
½ cup light cream
½ teaspoon almond extract
2 or 3 tablespoons Calvados
2 cups heavy cream (for garnish)

Peel the top inch of each apple. Remove the stem and core, leaving the bottom as intact as possible. Enlarge the interior space to about 1 inch. Rub the cut surfaces with lemon juice. Place the apples in a buttered baking dish with a few tablespoons of water, cover them with foil, and bake them in a preheated 350°F oven for about 15 minutes.

Meanwhile, cream the sugar and butter and add the ground almonds, egg, cream, and flavorings, mixing after each addition. Remove the apples after 15 minutes, take off the foil, and fill the apples with the frangipane mixture. Bake them, uncovered, until they are tender, about 20 minutes more. Serve the apples warm, with cream if you wish.

FOUR FAVORITE WINTER MENUS

II

Gâteau de Crêpes
Layered Crêpes with Smoked Salmon

Boeuf à la Ficelle, Sauce Moutarde et Sauce Raifort
Poached Beef with Warm Mustard Sauce and Horseradish Sauce

Aligot de Pommes de Terre
Potato and Cheese Purée

Salade de Saison
Mixed Green Salad

Fromage
Cheese (Époisses)

Tarte aux Poires Frangipane
Pear-Almond Tart Emily

Wine: A Chablis with the *Gâteau de Crêpes,*
a Clos-Vougeot with the main course,
then a Monbazillac with the tart

This is a menu that men always seem to enjoy, and my husband is no exception. Whether François is entertaining friends or business acquaintances on cold winter evenings, this is the menu he will most likely request.

Gâteau de Crêpes

Layered Crêpes with Smoked Salmon

Serves 8

1 cup flour
Pinch of salt
2 cups milk
1 egg
2 egg yolks
2 tablespoons butter, melted, plus 1 or 2 teaspoons
    unmelted butter
¼ pound smoked salmon
1 cup sour cream
2 or 3 tablespoons lemon juice, or to taste
Salt and freshly ground pepper

To make the crêpes, sift the flour and salt into a bowl and add the milk slowly, stirring constantly. Add the egg and egg yolks and mix well. Stir in the melted butter just before cooking the crêpe batter.

In a small, heavy skillet or crêpe pan, melt the remaining butter. Film the pan with crêpe batter, tilting the pan to distribute it evenly. When the crêpe is lightly browned on one side, flip it over to cook the other side. Stack the crêpes and cool them, then enclose them in a plastic bag until you are ready to use them. You may make them ahead and freeze them; defrost them before proceeding.

Cut the smoked salmon into slivers. Layer the crêpes in a springform pan, strewing a little smoked salmon over each one. When the pan is full or the crêpes are all used, wrap the pan in foil, place it in a preheated 350°F oven, and heat the crêpes through, about 20 minutes.

Remove the springform pan from the layered crêpes. Make the

sauce by gently warming the sour cream in a saucepan with lemon juice and salt and pepper to taste. Be careful not to boil the sauce. Cut the crêpes in wedges and serve them with the warm sauce.

Boeuf à la Ficelle, Sauce Moutarde et Sauce Raifort

Poached Beef with Warm Mustard Sauce and Horseradish Sauce

Serves 8 to 10

For the beef:
A 3¼-pound eye of round roast or tenderloin of beef (use two roasts if necessary)
* 3 quarts brown stock

For the **sauce moutarde:**
1 cup heavy cream
⅓ to ½ cup Dijon mustard
Freshly ground pepper
Salt (optional)

For the **sauce raifort:**
⅓ to ½ cup prepared horseradish
½ cup heavy cream, whipped
Salt (optional)

To prepare the beef:
Trim and tie the meat. Leave long strings that will extend out of the pot when the meat is submerged.

In a 5-quart stockpot, bring the brown stock to a boil. Lower the meat into the stock, making sure it is completely covered by the liquid. Bring the stock back to the boil over high heat, then reduce it to a simmer. Cook the meat, uncovered, for 25 to 30 minutes. It should be rare or medium rare.

Carefully remove the roast from the broth, using the long strings to lift it out. It is very important to let it stand for at least 15 minutes before carving. Remove the strings from the meat and carve it into slices about ¼-inch thick. Arrange the slices on a platter and garnish it with *sauce moutarde* and *sauce raifort*.

To make the sauce moutarde:
Heat the cream gently in a saucepan. Add the mustard, whisking constantly. Season to taste with pepper, and salt if you wish.

To make the sauce raifort:
Fold the horseradish into the whipped cream. Season the sauce with salt if you wish.

Aligot de Pommes de Terre

Potato and Cheese Purée

Serves 4 to 6

1½ pounds white potatoes
4 ounces (½ cup) cream
4 ounces (1 stick) butter
1 small clove garlic, crushed
About ½ teaspoon freshly ground pepper, or to
    taste
¾ pound Cantal cheese, or aged Swiss or Cheddar,
    grated

Peel the potatoes, cut them into 1-inch pieces, and cook them until tender in boiling, salted water. Drain and let them steam for a minute, then purée them in a blender or food processor just until mealy.

In a saucepan, bring the cream and butter to a boil with the garlic and pepper. Add this to the hot potato purée with the cheese, and process for about 1 minute, until the mixture is smooth and homogenous. It should be stringy. Serve immediately.

Alternative method: If you don't have a blender or food processor, cut the potatoes into ½-inch pieces and cook them with the garlic in boiling, salted water until tender, about 10 minutes. Drain them, mash them with a fork, and immediately add the cream, butter, pepper, and cheese. Whisk the potatoes vigorously while they are hot. They should be smooth and homogenous but have a stringy texture.

Tarte aux Poires Frangipane

Pear-Almond Tart Emily

Serves 8 to 10

My friend Emily Crumpacker developed this recipe, which is one of the best frangipane tarts I have ever tasted.

 * 1 recipe *pâte sucrée*
 3 large ripe pears
 Lemon juice
 ⅓ cup plus 2 tablespoons sugar
 ⅓ cup (5 tablespoons) butter
 1 egg
 1 egg white or yolk
 ⅔ cup (3 ounces) ground almonds, made from ½
       cup whole blanched almonds finely ground
       with 1 tablespoon flour
 ¼ teaspoon almond extract
 2 tablespoons kirsch
 ⅓ cup apricot jam, strained and heated

Prepare the tart shell by lining a 10-inch tart pan that has a removable bottom with *pâte sucrée*. Chill the shell for at least ½ hour.

Peel, core, and halve the pears. Rub them with lemon juice and set them aside. Using a food processor or an electric mixer, cream ⅓ cup of sugar and the butter, add the egg and egg white (or yolk), and mix. Add the ground almonds, almond extract, and kirsch; mix well.

Place the pear halves cut side down on a cutting surface and slice them into thin pieces horizontally, keeping the slices together. Pour the almond-cream mixture into the well-chilled pastry shell and fan out the pear slices on top, with the tops of the pears toward the center and the wider bottoms toward the outside. Use two pears to form a cross and fill in the spaces with the remaining pieces. Sprinkle the pears with the remaining sugar and bake the tart in the lower third of a preheated 350°F oven for 35 minutes. Then move it to the upper third and continue baking until it is puffed and browned, 15 to 20 minutes more. Cool it and glaze it with apricot jam.

FOUR FAVORITE WINTER MENUS

III

Tarte aux Champignons des Bois
Wild Mushroom Tart

Échine de Porc en Couronne
Crown Roast of Pork with Celery Root Purée

Salade de Saison
Mixed Green Salad

Poires Babette
Gratinéed Pear Custard

Wine: A Pomerol with the whole menu

This menu and the one that follows are two of my favorite menus for entertaining. I do not think you will find them difficult to execute. Either roast makes a splendid presentation, and both are easy to carve.

Tarte aux Champignons des Bois

Wild Mushroom Tart

Serves 6

* 1 recipe *pâte brisée*
  10 or 12 ounces fresh wild mushrooms
* ¼ cup *crème fraîche* or heavy cream
  3 eggs
  Salt and freshly ground pepper
  Nutmeg
  2 or 3 tablespoons butter
  ½ cup grated Parmesan and/or Swiss cheese

Line an 8- or 9-inch tart mold with the *pâte brisée*, then line the shell with foil, fill it with rice or beans, bake it in a preheated 350°F oven until the pastry is lightly golden, about 20 minutes. Remove the rice and foil for the last 5 minutes.

Wash the mushrooms in water to which you have added several tablespoons of vinegar and rinse them thoroughly under running water. Place the mushrooms in a heavy saucepan or skillet and cook, covered, over low heat until they render their liquid. After 10 minutes remove them and strain the liquid; you will need ½ cup of mushroom juice.

In a bowl, mix the ½ cup of juice from the mushrooms with the *crème fraîche* or cream and the eggs; season to taste with salt, pepper, and nutmeg.

Sauté the mushrooms in the butter over high heat until they are lightly browned and place them in the partially baked tart shell. Pour the custard mixture over them, sprinkle the tart with cheese, and bake it in a preheated 350°F oven until a knife inserted in the center comes out clean, about 20 minutes. Serve warm.

Échine de Porc en Couronne

Crown Roast of Pork
with Celery Root Purée

Serves 6 to 8

A crown roast of pork, about 14 to 16 ribs
Salt and freshly ground pepper
Dry sherry
Thyme
Sage or rosemary
1 cup water
1 cup dry sherry
6 pears, peeled and quartered lengthwise and
    rubbed with lemon juice
½ pound prunes
1 pound celery root, peeled and cut in 1-inch cubes
½ pound potatoes, peeled and quartered
6 to 8 tablespoons butter
½ cup cream
Salt and freshly ground pepper
1 cup small pearl onions, trimmed
½ teaspoon sugar

Have your butcher prepare a crown roast from the loin end. The rib chops should remain unseparated; allow two ribs per person.

About 3 hours before roasting, sprinkle the meat with salt and pepper, sherry, and the herbs. Marinate it until you are ready to roast it. Calculate the roasting time at 30 to 40 minutes per pound, and add 15 or 20 minutes' standing time before carving. Put the roast in a preheated 450°F oven and immediately reduce the heat to 350°F. Roast the pork to an internal temperature of 180°F as registered on a meat thermometer, or for the calculated amount of time. Remove it and let it stand.

Meanwhile, heat the water with the cup of sherry in a large

saucepan, add the pears and prunes, and simmer gently for 10 to 12 minutes, until the pears are just tender. Cool the fruit in the poaching liquid if you are not ready to serve. Reheat before serving.

To prepare the celery root purée, cook the celery and potatoes in boiling, salted water until tender, about 15 minutes. Drain them and allow them to steam dry for 1 or 2 minutes. Purée the celery and potatoes in a food processor or food mill. Add 4 or 5 tablespoons of soft butter and ½ cup cream; beat well, and season to taste with salt and pepper. Keep the purée warm or reheat it before serving.

Cook the baby onions in 2 or 3 tablespoons of butter and a little water until slightly transparent. Add the sugar and continue cooking, uncovered, until the water has evaporated and the onions are tender and lightly caramelized.

Deglaze the roasting pan with the cooking liquid from the fruit. Remove any grease and boil to reduce the sauce to 1 cup.

To serve, place the roast on a serving platter and fill its center with celery root purée. Garnish the platter with poached pears and prunes and glazed baby onions. Serve the meat hot, with the reduced cooking juices in a sauceboat.

Poires Babette

Gratinéed Pear Custard

Serves 6

1 cup sugar
3 cups water
3 or 4 pears
2 cups milk
⅓ cup plus 1 tablespoon sugar
6 egg yolks
2 tablespoons flour
2 tablespoons rum or pear brandy
2 tablespoons ground almonds (optional)
5 or 6 macaroons, crushed (about ⅔ cup)
Powdered sugar (for garnish)

To poach the pears, heat the sugar and water in a large saucepan. Peel, halve, and core the pears and immerse them in the syrup. Simmer for 12 to 15 minutes, or until they are just tender. Cool them in the syrup.

Bring the milk to a boil with 1 tablespoon sugar and remove it from the heat. Meanwhile, beat the egg yolks and remaining sugar with flour in another saucepan until they are thick and lighter in color. Pour the hot milk slowly over the mixture, stirring constantly. Return the mixture to heat, bring it to a boil, and cook, stirring, 1 minute. Remove the custard from the heat and flavor it to taste with rum or pear brandy, and ground almonds if desired.

Spread a thin layer of custard in a buttered ovenproof dish; top it with a layer of sliced pears, and sprinkle the pears with macaroon crumbs. Continue in this fashion, forming two or three layers, ending with a layer of custard sprinkled heavily with macaroon crumbs. (You may prepare the dessert a few hours ahead to this point.)

When you are ready to serve, dust the top with powdered sugar and heat the custard in a preheated 350°F oven for approximately 8 to 10 minutes, until it is hot and bubbly. Then run it under the broiler to brown the top. Serve hot or warm.

FOUR FAVORITE WINTER MENUS

IV

Timbale d'Huîtres au Cidre Sec
Oysters with Cider

Selle d'Agneau Polignac
Roast Saddle of Lamb with Onion Purée

Haricots Verts au Beurre
Buttered Green Beans

Charlotte Malakoff aux Noisettes
Hazelnut Charlotte

Wine: A Sancerre with the oysters, then a Médoc

Timbale d'Huîtres au Cidre Sec

Oysters with Cider

Serves 8

8 eggs
½ cup hard cider
2 quarts mussels, scrubbed
24 oysters
½ pound mushrooms, sliced
½ cup water
6 tablespoons lemon juice.
Salt and freshly ground pepper

For the sauce:
½ cup butter
2 tablespoons flour
1½ cups hard cider
Juice from mussels, oysters, and mushrooms
2 tablespoons cream
⅔ cup Calvados
Croutons (page 212, for garnish)
1 tablespoon chopped parsley (for garnish)

Hard-boil the eggs, shell them, and cut them in half lengthwise.

Cook the mussels in the ½ cup of cider, reserving the cooking liquid. Open the oysters and reserve the juice. Cook the mushrooms in the water with the lemon juice and salt and pepper to taste. Set aside the cooking liquid.

To make the sauce, melt the butter in a saucepan, add the flour, and stir until well blended. Add the cider and cooking liquids from the mussels and mushrooms and the juice of the oysters. Whisk constantly as you heat the sauce just to boiling. Add salt and pepper to taste. Allow the sauce to boil for 2 minutes and then remove it from the heat. Just before serving, add the cream and Calvados.

In a shallow ovenproof dish, arrange the egg halves with the mussels, oysters, and mushrooms, and pour the sauce over them. Cover the dish with aluminum foil and heat it in a preheated 400°F oven for 5 minutes. Serve the timbale garnished with fried croutons and chopped parsley.

Selle d'Agneau Polignac

Roast Saddle of Lamb with Onion Purée

Serves 8

A 5- to 6-pound saddle of lamb (whole sirloin
     portion with bone)
Salt and freshly ground pepper
Thyme
1 pound onions, peeled and thinly sliced
6 tablespoons butter
3 tablespoons flour
1 cup milk
Nutmeg
½ cup grated Swiss cheese

Preheat the oven to 425°F. Place the lamb in a shallow roasting
pan, sprinkle it with salt, pepper, and thyme, and place it in the
oven. Immediately reduce the heat to 350°F. After 30 to 35 minutes, remove the roast and let it stand for 15 to 20 minutes or
longer. It will not be done.

In a heavy saucepan, cook the onions slowly, covered, in 3
tablespoons of butter, until very tender, about 45 minutes. Melt
the remaining 3 tablespoons of butter in a heavy saucepan. Add
the flour and cook until foamy, 1 to 2 minutes. Add the milk,
bring the sauce to a boil, and cook, stirring constantly, until it
thickens. Season it to taste with salt, pepper, and nutmeg. Mix it
with the onions and set them aside.

Carve the roast and reconstruct it, spreading onion purée between each slice and on top. Cover it with grated cheese and bake
it for about 20 minutes in a preheated 375°F oven, to finish cooking the meat. If the top is not browned, place the roast under the
broiler at the end of the cooking time. The meat should be pink
and not overcooked.

Haricots Verts au Beurre

Buttered Green Beans

Serves 8

3 pounds green beans, washed and with ends
    snapped off
6 tablespoons butter
Salt and freshly ground pepper

Drop the beans into boiling, heavily salted water and cook, uncovered, until they are almost tender, about 12 minutes. Drain
them. Melt the butter in a large, heavy skillet and sauté the beans
for several minutes over medium-high heat to finish cooking
them. Season them to taste with salt and pepper.

Charlotte Malakoff aux Noisettes

Hazelnut Charlotte

Serves 8

* About 16 to 20 ladyfingers
  Rum
  1⅔ cups hazelnuts
  ¾ cup confectioner's sugar
  1 cup (2 sticks) unsalted butter, at room
      temperature
  1 cup heavy cream, whipped
  ⅔ cup granulated sugar or crushed sugar cubes
  ⅓ cup water, plus ¼ cup cold water

To prepare the mold:
Cut a circle of wax paper the size of the bottom of a 6-cup charlotte mold and place it inside. Trim enough of the ladyfingers into wedges to cover the bottom of the mold in a sunburst pattern, placing the curved sides against the bottom. Brush or sprinkle these ladyfingers generously with rum. To line the sides, dip the flat sides of the remaining ladyfingers in rum and place the curved sides against the mold. Trim the ladyfingers after lining the mold and save any extras and trimmings.

To make the filling:
Toast the hazelnuts and remove their skins while they are still hot by rubbing them briskly against one another in a dish towel or between two strainers, one nested inside the other. Pulverize the nuts in a food processor or blender with ¼ cup of the confectioner's sugar. In a bowl, cream the butter with the remaining confectioner's sugar until it is light and fluffy. Add the pulverized nuts and 2 tablespoons of rum and beat the mixture until it is well mixed. Fold the cream into the butter-and-hazelnut mixture.

To assemble the charlotte:
Pour the filling into the prepared mold and smooth the top. Cover it with the remaining ladyfingers and trimmings; split them if necessary to cover the charlotte. If the sides extend above the filling, trim them and add the pieces to the ladyfingers on top to fill in spaces. Brush the top with rum, cover the charlotte with foil, and chill the mold for at least 6 hours.

To make the caramel sauce:
Place the granulated sugar or crushed sugar cubes in a small, heavy saucepan, add ⅓ cup of water, stir briefly with a clean spoon to dissolve the sugar, and boil the syrup over high heat until it colors. When it is a medium golden brown (about the color of cocktail peanuts), remove it from the heat and pour in the cold water to stop the cooking.

To serve:

Unmold the charlotte onto a serving plate and peel off the wax paper. Pour some of the caramel sauce around the base of the charlotte and serve the rest separately. Sometimes a charlotte is presented with a ribbon tied around the outside, which you remove before serving.

SPRING

Lunch at the Shore
Two Dinners from the Sea
Easter at La Coquetterie
Three Menus for Spring Weekends
Dinner for Audacious Gourmets

Almost everyone has heard something about apple blossom time in Normandy, but in May the lilacs and rhododendrons are no less spectacular. Spring is also the best time to see the emerald richness of our fields and woods. Ferns grow miraculously fast, and there are carpets of violets, wild hyacinths, and anemones.

May keeps us busy in the garden, battling the grass that covers paths and steppingstones. Calves and lambs are born, the new cider is ready to drink, and it is a joy simply to breathe in the reviving country air after a winter in the city. I find myself spending hours in the woods, gathering wild mushrooms and dandelions.

Springtime inspires one to wander. With visiting friends, I like to celebrate the pauses between rain showers by driving in to Rouen, lunching at a country inn, or exploring our great stone abbeys. Monasteries were established in Normandy in the sixth century, and three of the most beautiful — Saint-Wandrille, Jumièges, and Bec-Hellouin — are very near La Coquetterie.

We sometimes interrupt our *vagabondage* for lunch at Monsieur Guèret's restaurant at the Hôtel de Dieppe in Rouen. Monsieur Guèret's family have been hoteliers for more than a hundred years, and he loves to talk about Normandy, its food, and the origin of some of our province's recipes. Often we drive through miles of green farmland to the sea. My children enjoy looking for shrimp at Varengeville or visiting the old cod-fishing town of Fécamp, where, at a little restaurant looking out over the busy port, we eat great bowls of fish soup, crabs, and mussels. There is a certain zest in everything we do at this time of the year, and it is reflected in our appetites.

LUNCH AT THE SHORE

Salade de Poivrons et de Fenouils
Roasted Pepper and Fennel Salad

Pot au Feu de Mer Tabouelle
Creamy Fish Stew with Mustard

Tarte aux Citrons
Lemon Tart

Wine: A Rosé de Provence with the whole menu

Pot au Feu de Mer Tabouelle is named for my friend Monsieur Tabouelle, who is the last independent mustard maker in France. He lives not far away in the little town of Caudebec-les-Elbeuf, where his family has made mustard for 115 years. When I asked him whether Dijon mustard was made in Normandy, he informed me of a royal decree, issued in 1532, forbidding all manufacturers outside the Duchy of Burgundy to use the name *Dijon*. Now, however, since France has entered the Common Market, any "white" mustard manufactured in France may be called Dijon.

Salade de Poivrons et de Fenouils

Roasted Pepper and Fennel Salad

Serves 6

2 red bell peppers
2 green bell peppers
2 yellow bell peppers
3 small fennel bulbs
½ cup olive oil
3 tablespoons red wine vinegar
1 tablespoon Dijon mustard
1 clove garlic, crushed (optional)
Salt and freshly ground pepper
¼ cup small black niçoise olives

Put the peppers on the rack of a broiler pan under a preheated broiler, about four inches from the heat. Turn them frequently as you roast them for 20 to 25 minutes, or until they are blistered and charred. Take them out, enclose them in a plastic bag, and let them steam until they are cool enough to handle. Starting at the stem end, peel the peppers and discard the stems, the ribs, and the seeds as you cut the peppers into quarters. Save their juice, if possible, to add to the vinaigrette.

Cut the fennel bulbs into quarters and simmer them in salted water until they are just tender, about 12 to 15 minutes. Drain them and refresh them in cold water.

To make the vinaigrette dressing, combine the oil, vinegar, mustard, and garlic, if you wish, in a small jar. Shake it well and season the dressing to taste with salt and pepper.

To serve the salad, arrange sections of fennel and peppers by color on a serving plate in a sunburst pattern or stripes, depending on the shape of the plate. Decorate them with olives. Drizzle them liberally with vinaigrette and marinate the salad for at least 30 minutes at room temperature before serving.

Pot au Feu de Mer Tabouelle

Creamy Fish Stew with Mustard

Serves 6

1 pound monkfish
1 pound shrimp
½ pound scallops
½ pound salmon, trout, pike, or crayfish

For the court bouillon:
2 tablespoons butter
1 carrot, sliced
1 onion, sliced
1 cup white wine
3 cups water
* A large bouquet garni
6 peppercorns

For the stew:
6 medium carrots, peeled and cut into sticks
6 medium turnips, peeled and cut into sticks
6 celery stalks, cut into sticks
6 leeks, well washed and cut into julienne strips
2 egg yolks
1 cup cream
1 or 2 tablespoons Dijon mustard
Salt and freshly ground pepper

Wash the scallops and shrimp, then wash the fish and cut it into large pieces.

To make the court bouillon, melt the butter in a saucepan and sauté the carrot and onion for 1 or 2 minutes. Add the wine, water, bouquet garni, and peppercorns. Simmer the liquid for 20 minutes, then strain it. Return it to the saucepan.

Cook the vegetables for the stew in the court bouillon until they are almost tender. Add the monkfish, let it cook 2 minutes, then add the salmon, scallops, and shrimp in stages, so all will be done at about the same time. When they are done, in about 8 to 10 minutes, strain the stew over a large saucepan or skillet and put the fish and vegetables in a soup tureen.

Over high heat, reduce the liquid by half, then remove it from the heat. In a bowl, mix the egg yolks, cream, and mustard. Slowly pour a ladleful of broth into the cream mixture, stirring vigorously, then pour the mixture into the bouillon, stirring constantly. Cook over low heat for about 2 minutes, until it has thickened a bit. Taste this sauce and season it with salt, pepper, and more mustard if you wish. Pour it over the fish and vegetables in the tureen and serve.

Tarte aux Citrons

Lemon Tart

Serves 8 to 10

```
* 1 recipe pâte sucrée
  5 lemons (6 if they are very small)
  1 envelope gelatin
  ⅔ to ¾ cup granulated sugar
  1 cup heavy cream, whipped
  ½ cup granulated sugar (for garnish)
  Rind of 1 lemon (for garnish)
  ½ cup whipped cream (for garnish)
```

Line a 10-inch tart pan with the *pâte sucrée*. Prick the bottom of the shell with a fork and chill it for 1 hour, then line the shell with aluminum foil, fill it with dried beans, and bake it in a preheated 375°F oven for 15 minutes. Carefully remove the foil and beans and let the shell cool.

Grate the zest of 2 lemons, then squeeze all 5 lemons and add enough cold water to the juice to make 1⅓ cups of liquid. In a small saucepan or heatproof dish, soften the gelatin in ⅓ cup of this liquid. Then dissolve the gelatin mixture over heat, stirring until no crystals remain and the mixture is clear.

In a bowl, mix the sugar with the remaining lemon juice and stir to completely dissolve the sugar. Add the gelatin and stir well. Chill until the mixture is partially set.

When the lemon-gelatin mixture has almost set, fold in the lemon zest and the whipped cream and pour the mixture into the tart shell. Chill the tart. Serve it with a crown of caramel angel hair or with rosettes of whipped cream and candied lemon peel.

To make caramel angel hair:
Moisten ½ cup granulated sugar with several tablespoons of water in a small copper pan. Cook it over high heat until it becomes medium brown; remove it from the heat. Suspend a broom handle or long dowel between two chairs and spread several sheets of newspaper underneath to protect the area. Holding two forks back to back or a whisk with the loops cut off about 1½ inches from the handle, dip the tines or points into the hot caramel mixture and trail threads of caramel back and forth over the handle or dowel. Gather these up and place them on top of the tart. Alternatively, form the angel hair over an oiled, inverted bowl of approximately the same diameter as the tart. Angel hair must be made at the last minute, as it melts quickly.

To make candied lemon peel:
Follow the directions above for making caramel. Peel the rind of a lemon with a zester. Blanch the rind for 5 minutes in boiling water and pour it into the browned caramel for 2 minutes, just to give it a shiny coating. Remove and cool before you garnish the tart.

TWO DINNERS FROM THE SEA

These two menus remind me of the colorful old harbor of Honfleur. The quay is lined with narrow sixteenth- and seventeenth-century houses, and small yachts and fishing boats bob about at their moorings. My favorite quayside restaurant serves langoustines balanced on their tails on a bed of seaweed, with their claws entwined as if they were dancing around on the platter.

I

Salade de Moules
Salad of Mussels and Celery

Poisson Farci au Cidre
Stuffed Flounder in Cider

Pain d'Épinards
Spinach Loaf

Gâteau au Chocolat Marie-Blanche, Crème Fouettée au Café
Marie-Blanche's Chocolate Cake with Coffee Whipped Cream

Wine: A Muscadet with the mussels and fish,
a Sauterne with the chocolate cake

Salade de Moules

Salad of Mussels and Celery

Serves 6

For the dressing:
1 tablespoon Dijon mustard
Juice of 1 lemon
½ cup oil
* ¼ cup *crème fraîche* or sour cream
1 cup minced chives and chervil, parsley, tarragon,
    or dill
Salt and freshly ground pepper

For the mussels:
2 quarts mussels
½ cup white wine
6 ounces small cooked shrimp
1 celery root, peeled and cut into large julienne
    strips or sticks
Juice of ½ lemon
6 stalks celery, sliced
1 head romaine or other firm lettuce

To make the dressing, combine the mustard and 2 tablespoons of lemon juice in a bowl. Slowly add the oil in a stream, stirring constantly. The dressing will thicken like mayonnaise. Mix in the *crème fraîche* or sour cream and minced herbs, and season to taste with salt, pepper, and the remaining lemon juice.

Clean the mussels, scrubbing them well, and steam them open over high heat in a heavy pan, covered, with the wine. When they have opened, drain them and remove the mussels from the shells, discarding any unopened ones. Combine the mussels with the cooked shrimp and half the dressing and set them aside.

Cook the pieces of celery root with the lemon juice in enough water to cover for about 10 to 15 minutes, until they are tender but not soft. Drain them and refresh them in cold water. Mix them with the sliced celery and remaining dressing.

To serve, place the celery on a bed of lettuce and pile the mussels in the center, or toss them to combine.

Poisson Farci au Cidre

Stuffed Flounder in Cider

Serves 6 to 8

8 large shallots, peeled
1 pound mushrooms, cleaned and trimmed
12 ounces whiting or sole, skin removed
3 large egg whites
Salt and freshly ground white pepper
1 cup heavy cream, chilled
½ cup chopped parsley
6 tablespoons (¾ stick) unsalted butter
A whole flounder, about 3½ pounds, cleaned
⅔ cup fresh white bread crumbs
1 bottle hard cider

Chop the shallots and set them aside. Chop the mushrooms coarsely and set them aside. Cut the whiting or sole into 1-inch pieces. Using a food processor, purée the pieces of fish for about 45 seconds, stopping as necessary to scrape the bowl. With the machine running, add the egg whites and process for 10 seconds. Add ½ teaspoon of salt and ½ teaspoon of pepper. With the machine still running, pour ½ cup of the cream through the feed tube in a thin, steady stream. Add 2 tablespoons of the chopped parsley and mix well. Refrigerate this mousseline mixture.

In a medium skillet, melt 3 tablespoons of the butter over moderate heat. Add the chopped mushrooms and ¼ cup of the chopped shallots and cook, stirring, until the mushrooms have released their moisture and it has evaporated. Remove the skillet from the heat and set it aside.

Butter a baking dish just large enough to hold the flounder. Lay the flounder on a counter with its dark side up. Using a sharp, flexible knife, cut down through the skin and flesh along the backbone, from the head to the tail. Holding the knife flat against the rib bones, separate the flesh from the backbone almost to the edge of the fish, to create a pocket. Do not cut through the side. Repeat this on the other side, cutting from the backbone almost to the edge. Bend the fish across the middle, with the bones facing out, to break the backbone. Lay the flounder out flat, with the slit side up, and remove the backbone and the attached rib bones in two sections. Sprinkle the pockets lightly with salt and pepper.

Using a pastry bag or spoon, fill the pockets with the cold mousseline mixture. Sprinkle the remaining chopped shallots over the bottom of the prepared baking dish. Carefully transfer the flounder to the dish. Spread the reserved mushroom mixture over the top of the fish, leaving the head and tail uncovered. Sprinkle with the remaining parsley and the bread crumbs and dot with the remaining butter. Pour the cider around the fish.

Bake the flounder in the center of a preheated 350°F oven for about 25 minutes, or until the fish is done and the mousseline is firm. Remove the baking dish from the oven. Tilting the dish, ladle the pan juices into a 2-quart saucepan. Set aside the baking dish and keep it warm.

Boil the juices over moderately high heat until they are reduced to ¾ cup. Strain them into a small saucepan and stir in the remaining ½ cup of heavy cream over moderately high heat. Boil the sauce until it is reduced to 1 cup.

Serve the fish from the baking dish and pass the sauce separately.

Pain d'Épinards

Spinach Loaf

Serves 6 to 8

1½ pounds fresh spinach, washed and with large
    stems removed, or 1 10-ounce package frozen
    spinach, thawed and drained
6 tablespoons unsalted butter
1 tablespoon unbleached all-purpose flour
¼ teaspoon freshly ground black pepper
⅛ teaspoon freshly grated nutmeg
1 cup milk
1 2-ounce can anchovy fillets, drained and rinsed
2 large eggs
4 large egg yolks
3 ounces Swiss cheese, grated
½ cup heavy cream
Freshly ground white pepper

Generously butter a 4-cup rectangular mold and set it aside.

If you are using fresh spinach, blanch it for 4 minutes in a large pan of lightly salted, boiling water. Drain and refresh it in cold water, then set it aside to drain again.

In a 1-quart saucepan, melt 2 tablespoons of the butter over moderately low heat. Stir in the flour, black pepper, and nutmeg until smooth. Add the milk all at once and whisk vigorously until the mixture boils, taking care to reach the bottom of the pan. Remove the saucepan from the heat and set it aside.

Press the fresh or thawed spinach between your palms to remove as much moisture as possible. Using a food processor, process the spinach and the anchovies until they are finely chopped. Add the eggs, egg yolks, reserved white sauce, and cheese and mix well.

Transfer the mixture to the prepared mold and bake it in the center of a preheated 400°F oven for about 30 minutes, or until a knife inserted in the center comes out clean. Remove it from the oven and let it stand for 5 to 10 minutes.

Meanwhile, in a small saucepan whisk together the cream, remaining butter, and a grinding of white pepper over moderately low heat until the sauce is hot and well blended.

Invert the mold over a serving plate, remove the spinach loaf from it, and pour the sauce over the top. Cut the loaf into ¾-inch slices to serve.

Gâteau au Chocolat Marie-Blanche, Crème Fouettée au Café

Marie-Blanche's Chocolate Cake with Coffee Whipped Cream

Serves 8

For the cake:
8 ounces semisweet chocolate
8 ounces (2 sticks) unsalted butter, at room
    temperature
1¼ cups sugar
5 large eggs

For the coffee whipped cream:
1 cup heavy cream, chilled
2 tablespoons confectioner's sugar
1 tablespoon strong coffee

To make the cake:
Butter a 9-by-1½-inch round cake pan. Line the bottom with wax paper and butter the paper.

In the top of a double boiler, melt the chocolate over hot water.

Add the butter and stir until the butter has melted and the mixture is smooth. Remove it from the heat for 1 to 2 minutes to cool slightly. Gradually whisk the sugar into the chocolate mixture; continue whisking until the mixture is thick and smooth, about 1 minute. In a separate bowl, beat the eggs until they are foamy. Then beat them into the chocolate mixture, just until they are well incorporated.

Pour the mixture into the prepared pan and place the pan in a 14-by-11-inch baking pan. Add enough boiling water to come halfway up the side of the cake pan. Bake the cake in the center of a preheated 350°F oven for 1½ hours, then remove the cake pan from the water and set it aside to cool to room temperature, about 1 hour. Refrigerate it until it is chilled, about 2 hours.

Run a knife around the inside of the cake pan, invert the chilled cake onto a plate, remove the pan and wax paper, and immediately invert the cake again onto a serving plate. Serve it with Coffee Whipped Cream.

To make the coffee whipped cream:
Beat the cream until it just begins to hold its shape. Sift the confectioner's sugar over the top and continue to beat until the cream holds soft peaks. Stir the coffee into the cream and refrigerate it until you are serving. Makes about 1½ cups.

TWO DINNERS FROM THE SEA

II

Mousseline de Crevettes
Molded Shrimp Mousseline

Poisson à la Rouennaise au Beurre Rouge
Fish Cooked in Red Wine with Red Butter Sauce

Pommes de Terre Polonaises
Potato Nuggets

Salade de Saison
Mixed Green Salad

Paris-Brest au Café
Choux Pastry Ring with Coffee Cream

Wine: A white Sancerre with the *Mousseline de Crevettes*, then a red Sancerre

Mousseline de Crevettes

Molded Shrimp Mousseline

Serves 6

For the mousseline:
1 pound shrimp, shelled
3 egg whites
¾ cup heavy cream
Salt and freshly ground pepper
Nutmeg
Lemon juice

For the sauce:
3 or 4 shallots, minced
1½ tablespoons butter
3 to 4 tablespoons white wine
1½ cups heavy cream
2 sprigs fresh tarragon or ½ teaspoon dried taragon

Drain the shrimp and pat them dry. Reserve 6 shrimp and place the rest in the work bowl of a food processor. Purée them, then add the egg whites one at a time, with the machine running. Add the cream by tablespoonfuls. Season the mousseline to taste with salt, pepper, nutmeg, and a few drops of lemon juice. Poach a spoonful in simmering water to check the seasoning and consistency, and rectify the seasoning if necessary.

Fill 6 well-buttered molds or custard cups with the mousseline. Lay a whole shrimp in the center of each mold. Bake the molds in a water bath in a preheated 350°F oven for about 15 minutes.

To make the sauce, sauté the shallots in the butter until they are transparent. Add a few tablespoons of white wine and boil for 1 minute. Pour in the cream and add the tarragon. Reduce the sauce by half and remove the tarragon sprigs before serving.

Unmold the mousseline onto individual plates and surround each serving with hot sauce.

Poisson à la Rouennaise au Beurre Rouge

Fish Cooked in Red Wine with Red Butter Sauce

Serves 6

Cooking fish in red wine is a very old Norman custom. Before 1450, while Normandy was under English domination, the English brought such quantities of red wine from Bordeaux that the Normans found ways to cook with it.

> A turbot or sea bass, about 4 pounds
> 2 shallots, peeled and chopped
> 4 leeks, chopped
> 2 tablespoons butter
> ½ bottle light red wine
> * About 2 cups fish stock
> * Bouquet garni
> 2 tablespoons heavy cream
> 4 ounces (1 stick) cold butter, cut in 12 pieces

Butter an ovenproof dish as close as possible to the size of the fish. The fish should be cleaned and scaled but left whole; remove only the tail and/or the head, if you must, in order to fit the fish into your pan.

In a skillet, gently sauté the shallots and leeks in the butter until they are transparent. Arrange them in the baking dish with the fish. Pour on the red wine and fish stock just to cover. Add the bouquet garni and cover the dish with foil. Bake the fish in a preheated 350°F oven, about 10 minutes per inch of thickness of the fish. Do not overcook. Remove the fish to a serving platter, wrap it in foil, and keep it warm.

Transfer the cooking liquid to a large saucepan and reduce it over high heat. When there is less than 1 cup, strain it into a small saucepan, add the cream, and continue reducing until you have 2 or 3 tablespoons. Remove it from the heat and add the butter one piece at a time, whisking vigorously. Do not reheat the sauce.

To serve, unwrap the fish, pour some sauce over it, and present the remaining sauce separately.

Pommes de Terre Polonaises

Potato Nuggets

Serves 6

1½ pounds very small new potatoes
3 tablespoons butter, melted
2 tablespoons finely minced fresh tarragon, chives,
    and chervil, or 1 teaspoon dried herbs
Salt and freshly ground pepper

Scrub the potatoes but do not peel them. Blot them dry and cut them in half. Mix the melted butter and herbs, heat them in a saucepan until foamy, and toss with the potatoes to coat them. Arrange the potatoes in one layer in a shallow baking dish and bake them in a preheated 425°F oven until they are crispy, about 20 minutes. Sprinkle them with salt and pepper and serve in a napkin-lined basket.

Paris-Brest au Café

Choux Pastry Ring with Coffee Cream

Serves 6

For the pastry:
⅞ cup water
4 ounces (1 stick) butter
Pinch of salt (more if you are using unsalted butter)
1 cup flour, sifted
4 large eggs
1 egg, beaten (for glaze)
Slivered almonds (for garnish)
Powdered sugar (for garnish)

For the pastry cream:
1 cup milk
3 egg yolks
⅓ cup sugar
2 tablespoons flour
2 teaspoons coffee extract
1 teaspoon vanilla extract
3 egg whites
Pinch of salt

To make the pastry:
Place the water, butter, and salt in a saucepan and bring them to a
boil. When the butter has melted, remove the pan from the heat and
add the flour all at once, beating well. Beat over moderate heat
for about 30 seconds to dry the mixture. Remove the pan from the
heat and add the eggs one at a time, beating very well after each
addition. (You may do this by hand or in a food processor.)

Using a dinner plate as a guide, outline a circle on a greased
baking sheet. Fill a pastry bag fitted with a large round tip with the
choux pastry. Following the outline, pipe two hollow circles, one

on top of the other. Lightly mark the top with the tines of a fork. Glaze the pastry with the beaten egg and sprinkle it with slivered almonds. In the center of the circle and around the edges, pipe some round choux about the size of whole almonds until you run out of pastry.

Place the baking sheet in a preheated 450°F oven and immediately reduce the heat to 350°F. Bake the ring for 25 to 30 minutes; dust the circle with the powdered sugar near the end of the cooking time. Remove the pastry from the oven and cool it.

Cut the small choux into quarters and split the circle in half crosswise to form two whole rings. Place the bottom circle cut side up on a serving plate.

To make the pastry cream:

In a large, heavy saucepan, bring the milk to a boil and remove it from the heat. In a large bowl, beat the egg yolks with the sugar and flour until they are light and fluffy. Pour the milk slowly into the egg-yolk mixture, stirring constantly, then pour the mixture back into the saucepan, return it to a boil, and boil for 1 minute, stirring vigorously. Flavor it with the coffee and vanilla extracts.

Beat the egg whites with a pinch of salt until they form stiff peaks. Fold them immediately into the hot pastry cream. The hotter the pastry cream is, the more stable the souffléed mixture will be.

To assemble the ring:

Spoon the souffléed pastry cream onto the bottom pastry ring. Place small pieces of choux around the edges to support the top. Spoon on more pastry cream and replace the top circle, cut side down. If you have a lot of pastry cream remaining, fill the center of the ring. Don't try to smooth the surface. You should assemble the ring close to serving time, as the pastry-cream mixture can collapse after 2 hours.

EASTER AT LA COQUETTERIE

*Oeufs Brouillés en Feuilletage
aux Pointes d'Asperges*
Scrambled Eggs and Asparagus in Puff Pastry

Gigot Parfumé aux Herbes Nouvelles
Leg of Lamb Marinated with Fresh Herbs

Gratin de Poireaux et de Pommes de Terre
Gratin of Leeks and Potatoes

Salade de Saison
Mixed Green Salad

Marquise au Chocolat, Sauce Café
Chocolate Charlotte with Coffee Sauce

Wine: Champagne with the first course and
dessert, a Bordeaux Graves with the lamb

At Easter our family is once again gathered together in the comfortable warmth of the dining room at La Coquetterie. My mother's collection of blue-and-white faïence de Rouen gleams from the special alcoves shaped to hold each piece of china upon the apricot-colored walls, and a fire crackles in the big stone fireplace. On the table are mossy baskets of orange azaleas, and in the center sits a white porcelain hen, as she has for countless Easters, surrounded by dozens of chocolate eggs. From the windows we look out over the meadows where newborn calves, too young to frolic, remain in their mothers' shadows. A new cycle has begun again, and we take great pleasure in this continuity with nature.

Oeufs Brouillés en Feuilletage aux Pointes d'Asperges

Scrambled Eggs and Asparagus in Puff Pastry

Serves 6

Perfectly scrambled eggs are a luxurious dish when presented like this. If you bake the buttery puff pastry shell in advance, you can assemble the dish in a matter of minutes.

* **About ½ pound puff pastry or demi-puff pastry**
  ¾ pound asparagus
  12 eggs
  2 tablespoons water
  Salt and freshly ground white pepper
  Tabasco sauce
  4 to 5 tablespoons butter
  1 egg, well beaten (optional)

Line an 8- or 9-inch tart mold that has a removable bottom with the puff pastry. Prick the interior of the pastry shell well with a fork and chill it for 1 hour before baking. Line the shell with foil, place beans or rice inside, and bake it in a preheated 400°F oven for 10 to 15 minutes. Carefully lift out the foil and beans, prick the interior again, and bake the shell for about 10 minutes more, or until it is golden brown. Cool it on a rack and remove the outside ring. You may make the shell several hours in advance.

Wash and trim the asparagus. If the stalks are larger than pencil-size, peel them from below the tip to the stem end. Cut the tips 3 inches long and set them aside. Cut the stalks crosswise into ½-inch pieces. Bring a saucepan of salted water to a boil, add the asparagus stalks, and boil them slowly, uncovered, for about 5 minutes, or until just tender. Remove them with a slotted spoon and drain. Bring the water back to a boil and add the asparagus tops. Repeat the boiling process and drain them.

Beat the eggs with the water and salt, pepper, and a few drops of Tabasco sauce to taste, until they are just blended. Melt 3 or 4 tablespoons of butter in a 9-inch skillet. Pour in the eggs and stir them over moderately low heat. When they slowly begin to thicken, stir them rapidly into soft curds. Remove the eggs from the heat immediately and stir in 1 or 2 more tablespoons of butter. If the eggs appear to have cooked too much, stir in the well-beaten egg.

Mix the reserved asparagus stalks with the eggs, spoon them into the pastry shell, and garnish by placing the reserved asparagus tips in a sunburst pattern on the top. Serve immediately.

Gigot Parfumé aux Herbes Nouvelles

Leg of Lamb Marinated with Fresh Herbs

Serves 6 to 8

The lamb must marinate for 36 hours before you roast it. It would be difficult to overdo the amount of fresh herbs you use to perfume the lamb; you may vary the combination any way you like and use as many herbs as you wish.

For the marinade:
Olive oil
2 cloves garlic, unpeeled and cracked
12 sprigs thyme, tarragon, or both
1 bay leaf, crumbled
6 sprigs rosemary
1 lemon, thinly sliced
2 teaspoons coarsely crushed pepper

A 5-pound leg of lamb
2 cloves garlic, cut in slivers
2 tablespoons butter, softened

For the herb butter:
8 tablespoons (1 stick) butter
½ teaspoon salt (if you use unsalted butter)
1 tablespoon lemon juice
Freshly ground pepper
3 tablespoons fresh tarragon leaves
2 tablespoons chives
2 tablespoons chervil or parsley leaves

Watercress (for garnish)

Two days before serving, spread out a large piece of heavy wax paper, foil, or parchment and brush it with olive oil. Leave the edges clean. Not more than an hour before starting to marinate the lamb (or the herbs will lose their flavor), gather the remaining ingredients for the marinade together. Place half of them on the paper; lay the lamb on top, and cover it with the remaining herbs and spices. Tightly close the paper around the lamb, but do not seal it so completely that it is airtight. Place the lamb in the refrigerator until you are ready to roast it.

A few hours before serving, remove the lamb from its marinating envelope and wipe it off. Insert the slivers of garlic into pockets you have cut all over the leg and spread the soft butter over the meat. Place the lamb on a rack in a roasting pan and roast it in a preheated 425°F oven for 15 minutes. Then reduce the heat to 350°F and roast for 1¼ to 1½ hours, or until a meat thermometer registers 160°F (for medium-done). Transfer the lamb to a warm serving platter and let it rest for 15 minutes before carving.

To make the herb butter, mix all the ingredients in a blender or food processor until they are well homogenized. Or you may chop the herbs by hand and mix them into the softened butter.

When you are ready to serve the lamb, dot it liberally with herb butter and garnish it with watercress.

Gratin de Poireaux et de Pommes de Terre

Gratin of Leeks and Potatoes

Serves 6

4 to 6 leeks
2 tablespoons butter
4 medium potatoes
½ cup milk
Salt and freshly ground pepper
Nutmeg
½ teaspoon dry mustard
½ teaspoon dried basil and thyme, or whatever you
    prefer
½ cup cream

Wash and trim the leeks. Slice them coarsely and sauté them in butter in a heavy ovenproof casserole over low heat until they have wilted. Peel the potatoes, cut them in thin slices, and add them to the leeks. Cover with milk, add the seasonings, and bake the casserole in a preheated 325°F oven until the vegetables are almost tender and most of the milk has been absorbed, about 20 minutes. Pour the cream on top and continue baking until the gratin is browned and the vegetables are done.

Marquise au Chocolat, Sauce Café

Chocolate Charlotte with Coffee Sauce

Serves 6

For the charlotte:
* About 18 or 20 ladyfingers
  Rum or Cognac
  8 ounces sweet chocolate
  2 ounces unsweetened chocolate
  ½ cup water
  3 tablespoons instant coffee powder
  ⅔ cup sugar
  5 egg whites
  1 cup heavy cream, whipped
  1 teaspoon vanilla extract

For the sauce:
1 cup milk
1 vanilla bean, cut into pieces
5 egg yolks
½ cup sugar
Coffee extract

To make the charlotte:
Split the ladyfingers lengthwise and sprinkle the cut sides with rum or Cognac. Line the bottom of an oiled 6-cup charlotte mold with wax paper. Trim enough ladyfingers in a teardrop shape to cover the bottom of the mold, placing the cut side up. Stand the remaining ladyfingers around the sides, with the curved sides against the mold. The ladyfingers should touch.

Cut the chocolate into pieces and place it in the top of a double boiler. Melt it slowly over low heat with ¼ cup of water and the instant coffee, stirring frequently, until it is smooth; set it aside.

Place the sugar and remaining ¼ cup of water in a heavy sauce-pan and boil over high heat until the syrup reaches the soft-ball stage, about 235°F on a candy thermometer. (If you don't have a thermometer, test the cooked sugar by putting a few drops into ice water. The drops should form soft balls when you roll them between your fingers.) Brush down the sides of the pan with water as necessary to dissolve any crystals. When the sugar has cooked enough, remove it from the heat.

In a large bowl, beat the egg whites with an electric mixer, starting slowly and gradually increasing speed until they form soft peaks. Pour the hot syrup in a stream into the egg whites and continue beating until they become stiff and glossy. Beat the whites until they have cooled to body temperature and gently fold in the melted chocolate and the whipped cream. Flavor with 2 or 3 tablespoons of rum or Cognac and vanilla. Spoon the chocolate mixture into the prepared mold and chill it for at least 4 hours.

To make the sauce:
Bring the milk to a boil with the vanilla bean. Meanwhile, beat the egg yolks and sugar until they are fluffy and lighter in color. Pour the hot milk slowly into the egg-yolk mixture, stirring vigorously, then pour the custard back into the saucepan and cook it over medium heat, stirring constantly, until it coats the back of a spoon and has thickened slightly. Add coffee extract to taste; strain and chill the custard. If a skin forms on top, strain it again before serving.

To serve:
Unmold the charlotte onto a serving plate and surround it with the coffee custard sauce.

Variation:
The charlotte filling may be served alone as a chocolate mousse.

THREE MENUS FOR
SPRING WEEKENDS

The joy of witnessing Normandy in the springtime must be shared. At La Coquetterie we enjoy opening the shutters, airing out the guest rooms, and otherwise preparing for friends who come to inhale the perfume of apple blossoms and wander through our beech woods gathering the first wild anemones. Spring inspires us to take a fresh look at everything, even Sundays at home. I love planning menus using tender new vegetables, veal, and duckling to honor the spring.

I: LUNCH

Potage de Petits Pois Frais
Fresh Pea Soup

Filets de Sole et Coquilles Saint-Jacques en Laitue
Fillets of Sole with Scallops on Lettuce Leaves

Asperges Sauce Maltaise
Asparagus with Orange Mousseline Mayonnaise

Polonaise
Individual Brioche Desserts

Wine: A Sauterne with the whole menu

Potage de Petits Pois Frais

Fresh Pea Soup

Serves 6

This soup loses its character if not made with fresh peas. If you cannot find fresh peas, you can easily substitute *Crème de Chou-Fleur* (p. 266) for this course.

For the soup:
4 pounds fresh peas
1 shallot or 2 scallions
* 2 cups chicken stock
1 to 2 teaspoons sugar
⅔ cup cream, or to taste
Salt and freshly ground pepper

For the croutons:
6 slices white bread
½ cup butter
½ cup oil

To make the soup:
Shell the peas and mince the shallot or scallions. Simmer these ingredients in the chicken stock with sugar until the peas are tender. Purée them in a food processor or blender or pass them through a food mill. Strain them in a medium-mesh strainer, pushing through as much purée as possible. Add the cream, heat the soup in a saucepan, and season it to taste with salt and pepper. To serve, sprinkle the soup with croutons.

To make croutons:
Cut firm white bread into ¼-inch cubes. In a small skillet, heat the butter and oil, which should be about ½ inch deep. When the oil

begins to smoke, add the bread cubes and fry them until they are golden, shaking the pan occasionally to brown them evenly. Drain them well on paper towels.

Filets de Sole et Coquilles Saint-Jacques en Laitue

Fillets of Sole with Scallops in Lettuce Leaves

Serves 6

6 sole fillets, about 6 ounces each, or 6 flounder
    fillets
6 sea scallops, washed
Salt and freshly ground pepper
About 12 large leaves of Boston lettuce
3 or 4 shallots, minced
⅓ cup white wine
2 tablespoons vinegar
2 tablespoons cream
4 ounces (1 stick) cold butter, cut into 8 pieces
Lemon juice

Pat the fillets and scallops dry and sprinkle them with salt and pepper. Roll each fish fillet around a scallop and secure them with toothpicks. Wash the lettuce, remove the center rib, and blanch one leaf at a time briefly in simmering, salted water until it wilts. Remove them from the water, carefully unfold the leaves, and spread them on towels to dry.

Butter a shallow baking dish just large enough to hold the fish; sprinkle it with shallots. Wrap each fish fillet in lettuce leaves and arrange them in the dish. Cover the dish with buttered foil and bake it in a preheated 350°F oven until the fish is just cooked, 15 to 20 minutes. Remove the fish to a serving platter, cover, and keep warm while you make the sauce. Reserve the cooking juices.

To make the sauce, pour the shallots and cooking juices from the baking dish into a small, heavy saucepan. Add the wine and vinegar and reduce the liquid over high heat until about 2 or 3 tablespoons are left. Add the cream and reduce it by half. Remove the sauce from the heat and add the butter one piece at a time, whisking constantly. Add the juice expressed by the fish while you have been making the sauce, and season with pepper and salt if desired, and a few drops of lemon juice. Do not reheat the sauce; it does not need to be very hot when you pour it over the fish.

Asperges Sauce Maltaise

Asparagus with Orange Mousseline Mayonnaise

Serves 6

2 pounds fresh asparagus (about 6 to 10 spears per
     person)
2 small oranges (blood oranges, if availabe)
3 egg yolks
About 1 cup vegetable oil
Salt and freshly ground pepper
Lemon juice (optional)

To prepare the asparagus:
If the spears are thin (pencil-sized), gently grasp each one with the tip end in one hand and the stalk end in the other and bend it until it snaps. Discard the stalk end; the spear will break at the point that it becomes woody. If you have large asparagus, peel each stalk from below the tip to the end, cutting more deeply toward the

end. You may tie the prepared asparagus in bundles for easier handling.

Steam or simmer the bundles in about 4 cups of salted water until they are just tender, 8 to 15 minutes, depending on size. If the spears are untied, simmer them not more than three deep in a large skillet. Serve the asparagus hot or warm with *sauce maltaise*.

To make the sauce:
Grate the zest from the oranges. Squeeze the fruit and heat the juice in a small saucepan. In a blender or food processor, beat the egg yolks with the orange zest. With the machine running, pour in the oil in a thin stream. When the mayonnaise is very thick, stop pouring in oil and add 1 tablespoon of boiling orange juice. With the machine running, add more juice, 1 tablespoon at a time, until the sauce is light and creamy. Season it with salt and pepper, and a little lemon juice if it is not tart enough.

Polonaise

Individual Brioche Desserts

Serves 6 to 8

At La Coquetterie we prefer our brioche for dessert, rather than for breakfast. A meringue-covered *Polonaise* filled with pastry cream and candied fruits is one of our most festive desserts.

For the brioche:
1 package active dry yeast
2 tablespoons very warm water
2 tablespoons sugar
2 cups flour
½ teaspoon salt (if you use unsalted butter)
3 eggs
4 ounces (1 stick) butter, softened

For the pastry:
1¾ cups flour
½ cup sugar
4 ounces (1 stick) butter
1 egg, beaten
2 or more tablespoons cold water

For the pastry cream:
1 cup milk
2 egg yolks
4 to 5 tablespoons sugar
2 tablespoons flour
½ teaspoon vanilla extract
½ cup candied fruit, finely chopped
½ teaspoon butter

For the syrup:
1¼ cups sugar
2 cups water
3 tablespoons rum or kirsch (optional)

For the meringue:
1¼ cups sugar
Water
4 egg whites

To make the brioche:
Dissolve the yeast in the warm water and add the sugar. Allow the mixture to stand for 5 to 10 minutes, until bubbles appear on the surface, to proof the yeast. Sift the flour and salt into a large bowl. Add the yeast mixture and eggs and mix until they are combined, then knead the brioche with a slapping motion against the sides of the bowl or on a marble surface. You may also use a mixer with a dough hook.

Incorporate the softened butter gradually into the dough, continuing to knead until the dough is smooth and elastic. Cover it and let it rise in a buttered bowl until doubled in volume, about 2 hours. Punch it down and roll it into small balls. Place these in well-buttered muffin tins or small molds; they should half-fill the molds. Let them rise until almost doubled, about 1 hour, then bake them in a preheated 425°F oven for 12 to 15 minutes. Cool them.

To make the pastry:
Combine the flour, sugar, and butter in a food processor or by hand until the consistency is mealy. With the machine running, pour in the beaten egg until the dough begins to form a ball. Stop the machine. By hand, mix in the cold water and gather the dough into a ball. Wrap and chill it for at least ½ hour before you roll it out to a ¼-inch thickness. Cut circles in the dough the same size as the bottom of the brioche molds. Bake them in a preheated 400°F oven for 8 to 10 minutes, until they are lightly browned.

To make the pastry cream:
In a large saucepan, bring the milk to a boil. Cream the egg yolks, sugar, and flour in a bowl or a food processor. They should be well mixed and lighter in color. When the milk boils, pour it slowly over the egg-yolk mixture, stirring vigorously. Return the mixture to the saucepan and stir vigorously over high heat until it comes to a boil. Remove it from the heat and stir briskly for another minute. Flavor the mixture with the vanilla and candied fruits, then place it in a shallow container to cool. When it is cool, rub the top lightly with butter and chill.

To make the syrup:
Combine the sugar and water in a saucepan. Bring the syrup to a boil and remove it from the heat. Flavor it with rum or kirsch if you wish.

To make the meringue:
Combine the sugar with enough water to dissolve it in a small pan; cook it until it reaches the soft-ball stage (225° to 240°F on a candy thermometer). Meanwhile, start beating the egg whites. When they form soft peaks, drizzle the cooked sugar onto them, beating constantly, and continue beating until the egg whites are cold and shiny.

To assemble the Polonaise:

Cut the brioches in half crosswise, brush them with syrup, and fill them with a layer of pastry cream. Place each brioche on a pastry base (stick it on with a little meringue if necessary). Frost the brioches completely with meringue and chill them for 1 or 2 hours, until you are ready to bake. Bake them for about 2 minutes in a preheated 450°F oven. (You may also prepare them well in advance and serve them cold.)

THREE MENUS FOR SPRING WEEKENDS

II: DINNER

Terrine de Truite Cressonière,
Mayonnaise au Cresson
Trout Terrine with Watercress Mayonnaise

Canard aux Navets Nouveaux
Duck with Young Turnips

Purée de Pommes aux Épices
Applesauce Spiced with Chutney

Fromage
Cheese (Vacherin)

Tarte à la Rhubarbe et aux Fraises
Rhubarb-Strawberry Tart

Wine: A Riesling with the trout, then a
Côte de Beaune

Terrine de Truite Cressonière, Mayonnaise au Cresson

Trout Terrine with Watercress Mayonnaise

Serves 6

For the terrine:
2 small salmon trout or Cohoe salmon, filleted
Salt and freshly ground pepper
8 ounces boneless firm white fish, such as pike,
    scrod, or halibut
1 cup watercress, blanched in salted water and
    squeezed dry
1 to 2 egg whites
⅓ cup cream
Nutmeg
Lemon juice
Allspice
Tabasco sauce or cayenne

For the mayonnaise:
1 small bunch watercress, washed and with stems
    removed
* 1 cup mayonnaise
1 tablespoon lemon juice, or to taste
Salt and freshly ground pepper

To prepare the terrine:
Cut the salmon trout fillets into lengthwise strips about ½-inch
wide. Sprinkle them with salt and pepper and set them aside on
paper towels.

Cut the white fish fillets into chunks, removing any bones you
find with your fingertips. Purée the chunks in a food processor or

blender. Add the watercress, which should be squeezed very dry. Purée the mixture until it is smooth; add 1 egg white and mix well. Chill the mixture in the freezer; when it is very cold, add the cream and season it to taste with the nutmeg, lemon juice, allspice, and Tabasco sauce or cayenne. The mousseline should be highly seasoned, as it is served cold. Poach a spoonful in salted, simmering water and test its consistency and seasoning. If it is too soft, add ½ to 1 more egg white; if it is too hard, add a little more cream.

Line a 3½- to 4-cup oiled loaf pan with buttered parchment or wax paper and layer about one-fourth of the mousseline into the bottom. Lay strips of salmon trout lengthwise on top (do not crowd them), and cover them with more mousseline; alternate layers, ending with the mousseline. Cover the terrine with buttered foil and bake it in a water bath in a preheated 350°F oven until a skewer inserted into the center comes out clean, about 30 to 35 minutes. Cool and chill it in the pan.

To make the mayonnaise:
Blanch the watercress in a large quantity of boiling, salted water until it has completely wilted, about 1 minute. Drain and refresh it under cold water, then squeeze out all the water and purée the watercress in a blender or food processor. Add the mayonnaise and mix well. Season it to taste with lemon juice, salt, and pepper.

To serve:
Unmold the trout terrine onto a serving platter. Thin the watercress mayonnaise with a little lemon juice and cream and decorate the terrine with a few spoonfuls; serve the rest in a separate dish.

Canard aux Navets Nouveaux

Duck with Young Turnips

Serves 6

2 ducks, 5 to 6 pounds each, with wing tips, neck,
    and giblets removed
2 pounds small young turnips, peeled
4 tablespoons butter
Salt and freshly ground pepper
¼ cup wine
1 onion, coarsely chopped
1 carrot, coarsely chopped
1 shallot, coarsely chopped
1 clove garlic, crushed
1 tablespoon flour
1 tablespoon tomato paste
* 2 cups chicken stock or duck stock
* Bouquet garni
1 tablespoon Cognac (optional)

Truss the ducks and roast them in a preheated 400°F oven until
done, about 1¼ hours. While they are roasting, cook the turnips
in a large saucepan in 3 tablespoons of butter and 2 or 3 tablespoons of water; add a little salt and pepper. When the water
evaporates, the turnips will begin to glaze. You may also add a few
spoonfuls of cooking juices from the ducks. When the ducks are
done, remove them to a serving platter and keep them warm.
Deglaze the roasting pan with a little wine, then strain and degrease the cooking juices.

Heat 1 tablespoon of butter in a large, heavy-bottomed saucepan and brown the chopped vegetables and the garlic with the
wing tips, necks, and giblets from the ducks, reserving the livers.
Sprinkle them with flour, cook 2 minutes, and add the tomato

paste, stock, salt and pepper, and the bouquet garni. Cook over medium heat, uncovered, about 20 minutes, until the liquid is reduced.

Mince the duck livers and place them in a strainer. Pour the stock mixture over the livers through the strainer into another container, pressing on the contents to extract all the juice. Add the degreased duck cooking juices and the Cognac, if you wish, pour the mixture back into the saucepan, and reheat.

When you are ready to serve, carve the ducks or cut them into serving pieces. Return to the platter, garnish with turnips, and top with a little sauce. Serve the remaining sauce separately.

Purée de Pommes aux Épices

Applesauce Spiced with Chutney

Serves 6

1½ pounds tart apples, peeled and quartered
Juice and grated zest of ½ lemon
⅓ cup water
Salt and freshly ground pepper
Mango chutney

Cook the apple quarters with the lemon juice and water until soft. Add the grated lemon zest and a little salt and pepper. By the tablespoonful, stir in the mango chutney to taste and rectify the seasoning, if necessary, before serving.

Tarte à la Rhubarbe et aux Fraises

Rhubarb-Strawberry Tart

* 1 recipe *pâte brisée*
  1 egg white
  1 pound pink spring rhubarb
  2 cups sliced strawberries
  ¾ cup sugar
  2½ tablespoons quick-cooking tapioca
  3 tablespoons red currant jelly
  12 medium strawberries (for garnish)
* *Crème fraîche*

Line a 10-inch tart pan that has a removable bottom with the *pâte brisée*. Prick the bottom of the tart shell with a fork and chill it for 1 hour, then line the shell with aluminum foil, fill it with dried beans, and bake it in the lower third of a preheated 425°F oven for 15 minutes. Carefully remove the foil and beans and brush the bottom of the shell with lightly beaten egg white. Bake the shell for 10 to 15 minutes more, or until it is golden. Cool it on a rack. Remove the outside ring and place the shell on a cookie sheet.

Wash and trim the rhubarb and cut it into slices about ½ inch thick. Mash the strawberries. In a lightly buttered casserole with a lid, combine the rhubarb, strawberries, sugar, and tapioca. Cover and bake the mixture in a preheated 400°F oven for 25 minutes, or until the rhubarb is just tender.

Let the mixture cool slightly and spread it in the tart shell. Bake the tart in a 400°F oven until the filling just begins to bubble, about 20 minutes. Transfer the tart to a rack and let it cool.

Melt the currant jelly in a small saucepan. Cut the remaining strawberries in half and arrange them in a circle around the outside edge of the tart; brush them with the currant jelly. Serve the tart at room temperature with a bowl of *crème fraîche*.

THREE MENUS FOR SPRING WEEKENDS

III: DINNER

Saumon Poché à l'Oseille
Poached Salmon with Sorrel

Rôti de Veau aux Morilles
Roast Veal with Morels

Salade de Saison
Mixed Green Salad

Fromage
Cheese (Brie)

Glace au Miel en Tulipes,
Sauce au Chocolat Amer Chaude
Honey Ice Cream "en Tulipes" with Hot
Bittersweet Chocolate Sauce

Wine: A Vouvray with the salmon,
then a Saint-Julien

Saumon Poché à l'Oseille

Poached Salmon with Sorrel

Serves 8

A 4-pound salmon, cleaned and scaled, or a sea
    trout
* About 4 cups fish stock or court bouillon
  2 pounds fresh sorrel or 8 ounces canned sorrel
  6 egg yolks
  12 ounces (3 sticks) butter, melted and cooled

Remove the head of the fish and reserve it. In a large fish poacher
or container with a lid, cook the salmon over very low heat with
enough fish stock or court bouillon to cover until it is done, about
2 hours. It should be barely hot, the surface of the liquid hardly
trembling. Remove the fish and keep it warm. Reserve the cooking liquid.

Wash the fresh sorrel or drain the canned sorrel and place it in a
nonstick skillet over low heat. Cook until it "melts." Remove it
from the heat and cool it slightly, then purée it in a food processor
or blender.

In a large saucepan, whisk the egg yolks with ¾ cup of the fish
cooking liquid over low heat until they begin to thicken. Add the
cooled melted butter slowly in a stream, whisking vigorously.
Incorporate the sorrel purée gradually, a little at a time, whisking
constantly, until the sauce tastes as acidic as you like.

When you are ready to serve, poach the fish head for 5 minutes
in the stock and place it on the serving platter to complete the
cooked fish. Pour some of the sauce over the fish and serve the rest
in a sauceboat.

Rôti de Veau aux Morilles

Roast Veal with Morels

Serves 8

A 3-pound roast of veal, tied (you may pierce it
    with morels and ham, if you wish)
5½ tablespoons butter
¼ cup oil
2 carrots, sliced
2 onions, chopped
½ cup white wine
1 cup water
* A large bouquet garni
    1 cup (1½ ounces) dried morels, soaked in hot
        water
Salt and freshly ground pepper
1 large cucumber, peeled, cut in half lengthwise,
    seeded, and sliced ¼ inch thick
Sugar
2 tablespoons cornstarch or arrowroot
¼ cup cream

In a heavy ovenproof casserole, slowly brown the veal roast on all
sides in 2 tablespoons butter and the oil. Remove it, add the
carrots and onions, and sauté until they are lightly colored. Return
the roast to the pan and add the wine, water, and bouquet garni.
Cover it tightly and roast it in a preheated 325°F oven until done,
about 1½ hours or until it reaches a temperature of 175°F on a
meat thermometer.

Drain the morels and strain them, reserving the liquid. Wash
them to remove any sand and sauté them in 1½ tablespoons
butter and a little salt and pepper until browned. In a saucepan,
cook the cucumber slices in 2 tablespoons butter and ¼ cup wa-

ter, with a pinch each of sugar, salt, and pepper. The water will evaporate and leave the cucumbers glazed. Set the vegetables aside and keep them warm.

When the roast is done, remove it to a serving platter and keep it warm. Strain the cooking juices into a saucepan, scraping the casserole well to remove the brown bits. Add the soaking liquid from the morels strained through a coffee filter or several layers of cheesecloth. Reduce the liquid by one-third. In a separate bowl, mix the cornstarch or arrowroot and cream. Stir this mixture into the cooking juices and boil for about 2 minutes, until the sauce has thickened slightly.

Slice the roast, garnish it with the vegetables and a little sauce, and pass the remaining sauce in a sauceboat.

Glace au Miel en Tulipes,
Sauce au Chocolat Amer Chaude

Honey Ice Cream "en Tulipes"
with Hot Bittersweet Chocolate Sauce

Serves 6

For the ice cream:
1½ cups heavy cream
1½ cups milk
⅓ cup honey
6 egg yolks
⅓ cup sugar
Vanilla extract (optional)
1 egg white (optional)

For the tulipes:
7 tablespoons butter
½ cup sugar
3 egg whites
1 teaspoon vanilla extract
2 tablespoons cream
1 cup flour

For the sauce:
10 ounces semisweet chocolate
2 ounces unsweetened chocolate
½ to ⅔ cup hot water
1 teaspoon vanilla extract or 1 tablespoon Grand
    Marnier, rum, or any desired liqueur

To make the ice cream:
Place the cream, milk, and honey in a saucepan and bring them
gently to a boil. In a bowl, beat the egg yolks and sugar with a

whisk or an electric mixer until they are thick and light in color. When the milk has come to a boil, remove it from the heat and pour it slowly over the yolks, stirring constantly. Return the mixture to the saucepan and cook gently over medium heat, stirring constantly, until the custard mixture coats the back of a spoon, about 5 minutes. Strain the custard into a bowl set over ice and chill until it is cold, stirring frequently. Add vanilla to taste, if you wish.

Freeze the ice cream according to the instructions that accompany your electric or hand-cranked ice-cream maker. If you want to freeze it without using an ice-cream maker, add an egg white to the honey custard when it is cold. (The egg white will prevent crystals from forming.) Freeze the custard. When it reaches the consistency of ice cream, remove it from the freezer and beat it with a whisk until it is smooth and fluffy. Place it in a mold lightly greased with oil and freeze it again until you are ready to serve.

To make the tulipes:
Cream the butter and sugar in a blender or food processor or with an electric mixer until they are fluffy and light. Add the egg whites, vanilla, and cream; blend quickly. Sift the flour over the batter and fold to mix.

Grease several cookie sheets and mark on each one four or five circles about 4 inches in diameter, spaced widely apart. Place a heaping tablespoonful of batter on each circle and spread it with the back of a spoon or spatula to fit the circle. Bake the cookies in a preheated 425°F oven until they are brown around the edges, about 5 minutes.

Remove the cookies from the oven and immediately form the warm, pliable dough into cup shapes by placing each cookie in an oiled custard or tea cup and pressing it in with your hand or a smaller cup. If the cookies harden on the sheet before you can form them, return them to the oven to soften.

You can make the *tulipes* several days before serving; the recipe makes about 12 cookie dessert cups. (You may note that the batter is the same as for *Langues de Chat*, p. 237. The only difference is the special form the cookies take.)

To make the sauce:

Cut the chocolate into small pieces. Over very low heat in a water bath or in the top of a double boiler, melt the chocolate, stirring frequently. When it is smooth and completely melted, add the hot water and thin the sauce to the desired consistency. Flavor it with vanilla or liqueur.

To serve:

Shaping the ice cream with a spoon, put three or four ice-cream balls into each of the *tulipes*. Pour some of the chocolate sauce over them. Serve the remaining sauce in a sauceboat.

DINNER FOR
AUDACIOUS GOURMETS

Salade de Pissenlit aux Lardons
Dandelion and Bacon Salad

Rognons de Veau aux Baies de Genièvre
Veal Kidneys with Juniper Berries

Pâtes Fraîches aux Herbes
Green Noodles with Herbs and Cream

Glace au Gingembre Frais
Fresh Ginger Ice Cream

Langues de Chat
Cat's Tongue Cookies

Wine: A Beaujolais Moulin-à-Vent with the
whole menu

I sometimes like to startle good friends with a piquant and unexpected menu. However, since everyone does not share the French enthusiasm for innards, you would be wise to determine how adventurous your gourmets are before offering them this zesty meal.

Salade de Pissenlit aux Lardons

Dandelion and Bacon Salad

Serves 4

In Normandy there are plenty of dandelions in the meadows around us in the spring, and we like to bring some home from time to time. We are careful to choose only very young plants that have not begun to flower, because after the plant flowers its leaves are tough and bitter.

This salad must be prepared just before serving, and you should warm the bowl or the bacon fat will congeal.

> 1 pound young dandelion greens
> 4 ounces slab bacon, sliced
> 1 tablespoon olive oil
> 2 tablespoons wine vinegar
> Salt and freshly ground pepper
> 2 hard-boiled eggs, yolks and whites sieved
> > separately.

Thoroughly wash and dry the dandelion greens. Cut the slab bacon into ½-inch pieces, cover it with cold water in a saucepan, bring it to a boil, and simmer for 5 minutes. Drain the bacon. In a skillet, sauté the bacon in the olive oil until it is crisp.

Fill a warmed salad bowl with the dandelion greens. Pour the bacon pieces and the fat over the greens. Add the vinegar to the skillet and over low heat stir in any brown bits that may cling to the bottom of the pan. Pour the vinegar over the salad and toss. Season the salad with very little salt and a good amount of pepper, and sprinkle the sieved hard-boiled eggs on top. Serve at once.

Variation:
You may use chicory or curly endive for this salad. However, be sure to remove any leaves that are too green or too tough.

Rognons de Veau aux Baies de Genièvre

Veal Kidneys with Juniper Berries

Serves 4

2 veal kidneys, peeled
3 tablespoons butter
¼ to ⅓ cup gin
¼ cup cream
* ½ cup brown or beef stock
1 tablespoon juniper berries, crushed
Salt and freshly ground pepper

Trim any fat from the veal kidneys and remove any remaining skin. Heat the butter in a skillet until foamy and add the kidneys. Cook about 4 minutes on each side; they should be quite pink inside. Add the gin, flame it, and remove the kidneys. Add the cream and stock to the pan and reduce the liquid by half, adding half the crushed juniper berries. Season the sauce well with salt and pepper.

Slice the kidneys into fairly large pieces and return them to the sauce to warm. Do not overcook them or they will become rubbery. Sprinkle the kidneys with the remaining juniper berries and serve them on a bed of green noodles.

Variations:
In place of the juniper berries and gin, flame the dish with Cognac or brandy and add 4 ounces sliced mushrooms sautéed in butter to the sauce before serving.

You may use the same method to prepare calf's liver or sweetbreads. Calf's liver requires about 1 minute per side in a hot skillet; slice it and serve as described for kidneys. Sweetbreads need to be soaked in several changes of cold water for about 2 hours; then blanch them by placing them in cold water to cover with 1 teaspoon salt and 1 tablespoon lemon juice and simmering for 15 minutes. For a neater appearance, press the blanched sweetbreads under a weight until they are well cooled. Sauté them for about 3 minutes per side and proceed as for kidneys.

Pâtes Fraîches aux Herbes

Green Noodles with Herbs and Cream

Serves 4

For the dough:
3 cups flour
¾ cup fresh chervil, leaves only
1 teaspoon salt
3 eggs plus enough water to make a scant ¾ cup
2 teaspoons oil

For the sauce:
½ cup chopped fresh tarragon, chives, and chervil,
     or your choice)
1½ cups cream
Salt and freshly ground pepper
Nutmeg

To make the pasta dough, combine 2¾ cups of flour, the chervil, and the salt in a food processor for about 1 minute. Add the egg mixture and oil and process for about 1 minute longer, adding the remaining flour by tablespoonfuls as necessary to cause the dough to form a ball and be fairly uniform green. It should not be sticky. Wrap the dough and chill it for about ½ hour (or 15 minutes in the freezer) before rolling it out.

Divide the dough into quarters. Roll it out very thin a quarter at a time, and cut it into narrow strips. If you are using a pasta machine, follow the manufacturer's instructions for rolling and cutting the dough. Sprinkle the noodles lightly with flour or cornmeal and spread them in a single layer to dry for at least 15 minutes before cooking.

To make the sauce, combine the herbs and cream and season to taste. Simmer the sauce, uncovered, until it has reduced by one-quarter.

Meanwhile, bring a large quantity of salted water to a boil with a tablespoon of oil in a large pot. Gradually add the noodles, maintaining the boil. Cook the pasta just until done, and drain it. Toss the noodles with the hot sauce and serve them sprinkled with freshly ground pepper.

Glace au Gingembre Frais

Fresh Ginger Ice Cream

Makes about 3 cups

6 egg yolks
⅔ cup sugar
⅓ cup water
1½ cups heavy cream, whipped
3 tablespoons very finely grated fresh ginger
¼ cup dark rum, or to taste

Put the egg yolks into a mixing bowl and have the electric mixer ready. In a small, heavy pan, dissolve the sugar in the water and boil it without stirring over high heat until it reaches the soft-ball stage (235° to 245°F on a candy thermometer). If you do not have a thermometer, you can test the syrup by putting a few drops into ice water; you should be able to roll them into a ball with your fingers and press the ball flat without much resistance.

Start beating the egg yolks. Pour the boiling sugar mixture over the yolks in a stream, beating constantly. (Avoid pouring the syrup directly onto the beaters.) The yolks will thicken and increase in volume. Continue beating until they are cool, about 15 minutes. It is helpful to beat them over ice after the first 5 minutes.

When the egg-yolk mixture is cold, fold in the whipped cream, ginger, and rum. Freeze the ice cream in a 3-cup mold or container.

Variation:
Glace aux Pistaches (Pistachio Ice Cream): Omit the rum and ginger. Add ⅓ cup blanched, peeled, and ground pistachio nuts to the sugar syrup and proceed as above, bringing the mixture back to the correct temperature before pouring it onto the egg yolks. Add vanilla extract, to taste, with the cream.

Langues de Chat

Cat's Tongue Cookies

7 tablespoons butter
½ cup sugar
3 egg whites
1 teaspoon vanilla extract
2 tablespoons cream
1 cup flour
4 ounces semisweet chocolate (optional)

Cream the butter and sugar in a blender or food processor or with an electric mixer until they are fluffy and light. Add the egg whites, vanilla, and cream; blend quickly. Sift the flour over the batter and fold it to mix.

Using a pastry bag fitted with a flat tip, pipe strips of batter about 3 inches long onto a greased cookie sheet. Leave at least the width of two fingers between the strips, as the dough will spread. Bake the cookies in a preheated 425°F oven until they are brown around the edges, about 5 minutes. Remove and cool them.

If you would like a chocolate garnish, cut the chocolate into pieces and melt it over very warm water over low heat, stirring occasionally, until it is smooth. Dip one end of each cookie in the chocolate. Let the cookies sit for a few minutes to harden the chocolate.

BASIC
RECIPES

BROTHS AND STOCKS

Freshly made stocks do not keep particularly well, so you should use them within two or three days, or freeze them.

Court Bouillon

Fish-Poaching Broth

Makes about 1 quart

> 1½ cups white wine or dry vermouth
> 2½ cups water
> 1 carrot, sliced
> 1 onion, sliced
> 1 or 2 shallots, sliced (optional)
> * Bouquet garni
> 8 peppercorns
> ½ teaspoon salt

Place all the ingredients in a large saucepan (preferably not an aluminum one), bring them to a boil, and simmer, covered, for about 30 minutes, after which time the court bouillon is ready to use for poaching fish or shellfish. Strain it if you wish.

Fond Brun

Brown Stock

Makes about 1 quart

Fond Brun is interchangeable with beef stock, which is made in the same way and can be substituted for it in any of the recipes.

> 4 to 5 pounds veal bones, or half beef and half
>   veal bones, cracked
> 2 large onions, cut in eighths
> 2 large carrots, cut in 1-inch pieces
> 2 celery stalks, cut in 1-inch pieces
> 10 peppercorns
> 3 allspice berries
> 2 or 3 cloves garlic, unpeeled
> * Bouquet garni
> 1 tablespoon tomato paste
> 1 or 2 beef bouillon cubes (optional)

Place the bones in a roasting pan and brown them in a very hot preheated oven (425°–450°F) for 30 to 40 minutes, stirring occasionally. Add the vegetables after 20 minutes and brown them also. When the bones and vegetables are well browned, transfer them to a stockpot and cover with water. Add the remaining ingredients and bring the stock to a boil, skimming the foam from the surface as it collects. Reduce the heat and simmer the stock, uncovered, for 4 to 5 hours, skimming as necessary, until it is well flavored. Strain and cool it and degrease it before you use or freeze it. You can remove fat most easily from chilled stock, as it congeals on the surface and can be lifted or spooned off.

Fond "Fantaisie"

Stock from Bouillon Cubes

Makes about 1 quart

2 onions, very coarsely chopped
2 carrots, cut into 1-inch pieces
2 stalks celery, cut into 1-inch pieces
2 tablespoons butter
5 cups water
* A large bouquet garni
8 peppercorns
Bouillon cubes (chicken and/or beef flavor)

To make an emergency stock without bones, sauté the vegetables in butter until they are very lightly browned. Add the water, bouquet garni, and peppercorns and the quantity of bouillon cubes appropriate for 1 quart of water: either chicken or beef flavor, according to your purpose, or some of each. Bring the stock to a boil, stir it well to dissolve the cubes, and simmer it, uncovered, for about 30 minutes. Strain and degrease the stock if necessary.

I find that Knorr brand bouillon cubes have the best flavor and are the least salty of those I have tried.

Fond de Volaille

Chicken Stock

Makes about 1 quart

1 pound veal bones, washed well (optional)
3 pounds chicken bones, including some with
  meat (such as necks and backs), or a whole
  fowl
2 small onions, sliced or coarsely chopped
2 small carrots, sliced or coarsely chopped
1 large stalk celery, cut in pieces
10 peppercorns
3 allspice berries (optional)
* Bouquet garni
1 or 2 chicken bouillon cubes (optional)

Place all the ingredients in a large pot. Cover them with water and bring the stock to a boil, skimming the foam from the surface as it collects. Reduce the heat and simmer for 3 to 4 hours, skimming as necessary. If you are using a whole fowl, remove it after 1½ hours, remove and reserve the meat, and return the carcass to the stockpot. When the flavor of the broth is sufficiently strong, strain and cool the stock. Degrease it before you use or freeze it.

 You may use the carcasses of one or two roasted chickens in place of some of the bones. The finished stock will be darker in color.

Fond de Canard

Duck Stock

Makes about 2 cups

1 duck carcass, including wings, neck, and back
2 tablespoons butter
1 carrot, roughly chopped
2 onions, roughly chopped
3 to 4 cups chicken broth
* Bouquet garni

Cut the carcass into pieces. Melt the butter in a large saucepan or stockpot and brown the carrot and onion pieces lightly, then add the duck pieces and brown them for a few minutes with the *mirepoix*. Add chicken broth to cover, and the bouquet garni. Bring the stock to a boil, then turn down the heat and simmer the stock, covered, for 1 hour. Strain before using.

Fumet de Poisson

Fish Stock

Makes about 1 quart

1 to 1½ pounds fish bones and heads
1 to 2 tablespoons butter
1 onion, sliced
1 small carrot, quartered
1 cup dry white wine
4 cups water
10 peppercorns
Pinch of salt
* Bouquet garni

Cut the fish skeletons into 3- to 4-inch pieces. Wash them well under cold running water with the fish heads, if any, to remove the blood. Drain.

In a large saucepan, sauté the fish bones and heads in butter with the onion and carrot over medium heat for about 5 minutes. Then add the wine, water, peppercorns, salt, and bouquet garni. Bring the mixture to a boil and reduce it to simmer, uncovered, skimming the foam from the surface as it collects. Simmer the stock for 20 minutes, then strain it. If the flavor is not strong enough, reduce it to concentrate the flavor.

Variation:
To make fish stock when you have no bones, substitute 2 cups of bottled clam juice for the bones and reduce the wine to ⅔ cup and the water to 2 cups. Sauté the vegetables in butter without browning them. Add the other ingredients and simmer, uncovered, for 30 to 40 minutes. Replace the salt with half a chicken bouillon cube, if you wish.

SAUCES AND SEASONINGS

Beurre Clarifié

Clarified Butter

Makes about ¾ cup

8 ounces (2 sticks) butter, preferably unsalted

Melt the butter in a small skillet or saucepan and cook it until it looks translucent but not brown under the foam. Skim off the white foam with a spoon. Pour the butter through several layers of cheesecloth placed in a strainer. If there is a milky white residue at the bottom of the pan, discard it.

Clarified butter may be heated to a much higher temperature than regular butter.

Bouquet Garni

A bouquet garni is a small bundle of aromatic herbs used to flavor various dishes. The basis for a bouquet garni is parsley leaves and stems, sprigs of dried thyme, and a bay leaf. Interesting additions include leek greens, celery leaves or stalks, and sprigs of other herbs that are included in the recipe for the dish you are making.

Tie the ingredients together in a bundle about 3 to 4 inches long, using the outside layer as a sort of covering, if possible. For instance, hold the parsley and thyme sprigs together, wrap them with a piece or two of leek greens and a bay leaf, and circle the bundle with string along its entire length. Tie it securely.

If you don't have sprigs of herbs, tie the ingredients in a small piece of fine cheesecloth.

Crème Fraîche

Makes 1 cup

1 cup heavy cream
1 tablespoon buttermilk

Place the cream and buttermilk in a jar, cover it tightly, and shake the mixture well. Let the mixture stand partially covered at room temperature for about 8 hours, or until it is thick. The *crème fraîche* keeps for four weeks in the refrigerator.

Sauce Beurre Blanc

White Butter Sauce

Makes about 1 cup

2 large or 3 small shallots, minced
3 tablespoons dry white wine
3 tablespoons white wine vinegar
* 1 tablespoon *crème fraîche* or heavy cream
6 to 8 ounces (1½ to 2 sticks) cold butter, cut in
    tablespoons
Salt and freshly ground pepper
Lemon juice (optional)

Combine the shallots, white wine, and wine vinegar in a small, heavy saucepan. Boil to reduce the liquid to about 1 tablespoon; add the *crème fraîche* or cream and reduce the sauce again to 1 tablespoon. Remove the pan from the heat and turn the burner to low.

Add the cold butter pieces one at a time to the sauce, whisking constantly. Return the pan to the heat occasionally as you add the butter pieces, working both on and off the heat so you can incorporate the butter without actually melting it. The mixture will become quite thick. When all the butter is incorporated, season the sauce to taste with salt, pepper, and a few drops of lemon juice if you wish. If it is too thick, thin it with a little hot water.

It is difficult to keep this sauce without melting the butter and causing the mixture to separate. Make it as close to serving time as possible. You may keep it warm in the top of a double boiler over water the temperature of a baby's bath.

Variation:
If you are serving the sauce with fish, add 2 or 3 tablespoons of concentrated, reduced fish stock to the sauce just before serving.

Sauce Hollandaise

Makes about 1 cup

> 3 egg yolks
> 1 tablespoon lemon juice, or to taste
> 6 ounces (1½ sticks) butter, melted and cooled
> Salt and freshly ground pepper

In a small, heavy saucepan, combine the egg yolks and 1 tablespoon each of water and lemon juice. Whisk until the mixture is frothy, then place it over very low heat and whisk until it has thickened, removing the pan from the heat at intervals so the bottom of the pan never becomes too hot to touch. With the pan off the heat, add the butter by drops, whisking constantly. After incorporating about half the butter, you may add the rest in a thin stream, as long as it incorporates into the sauce easily. If there is a milky residue at the bottom of the butter, do not add it to the sauce. Season the sauce to taste with salt, pepper, and more lemon juice. You may keep it until serving time in the top of a double-boiler over warm (never hot) water.

Sauce Béarnaise

Makes about 1 cup

3 tablespoons white wine
3 tablespoons wine vinegar
1 tablespoon minced fresh tarragon leaves or sprigs
2 shallots, minced
3 egg yolks
6 ounces (1½ sticks) butter, melted and cooled
Salt and freshly ground pepper

Combine the wine, vinegar, tarragon, and shallots in a small sauce-pan and bring the liquid to a boil. Continue boiling until the liquid has reduced to 2 tablespoons, then remove it from the heat. Strain and cool it.

In a separate saucepan, beat the egg yolks lightly, then add the reduced liquid and whisk until the ingredients are frothy. Place the saucepan over very low heat and continue whisking until the sauce has thickened, being careful not to overheat the bottom of the pan. With the pan off the heat, add the butter by drops, whisking constantly, until it is all incorporated. Season the sauce to taste with salt and pepper.

SALADS AND DRESSINGS

Salade de Saison

Mixed Green Salad

Salads should appeal to the eye as well as to the palate. I like to mix two or three shades of green and sharp flavors with sweet ones. Even in the middle of winter you can find romaine to provide some contrast to head lettuce, and perhaps you might add a little finely shredded red cabbage.

In France a green salad tends to be quite simple and is traditionally dressed with oil and vinegar. If you are using Boston lettuce, reconstructing the head in the salad bowl after you wash the lettuce and tossing it at the table is very attractive. Even a spoonful of chopped fresh herbs sprinkled on your salad will provide the necessary element of contrast. Don't forget wild greens such as young dandelion greens, watercress, lamb's lettuce, and so forth, which vary with the season and locality.

Greens can be washed several days ahead of time, spun dry, and arranged in a single layer on towels. Top them with another towel and roll them up loosely. Store the greens in a large plastic bag. To serve lettuce, snap off the tip of each stem and tear the leaves into bite-sized pieces, if you wish.

To estimate the proper quantity for a large gathering, count a handful of greens per serving. If your salad is to wait on the table before being tossed, make the dressing in the salad bowl, leave it in the bottom, and fill the bowl with greens. When you are ready to serve, turn the greens gently to coat the leaves with dressing.

Sauce Mayonnaise

Makes about 1¾ cups

1 egg yolk, at room temperature
1 egg, at room temperature
1 to 2 tablespoons distilled white vinegar
2 teaspoons Dijon mustard or ½ teaspoon dry
    mustard
1½ cups vegetable or peanut oil
Salt and freshly ground pepper

To make mayonnaise in a food processor:
Place the yolk, egg, and mustard with 1 tablespoon vinegar in the work bowl. Process for 1 minute and add the oil by drops. Some machines have a hole in the bottom of the pusher for this purpose. If not, pour the oil through the feed tube in a very thin stream. Season the sauce to taste with more vinegar, salt, and pepper.

To make mayonnaise by hand:
Use 2 egg yolks, reserving the whites for another purpose. Whisk the yolks with the mustard in a small mixing bowl set in a pan of very warm water, until they are well combined and the bottom of the bowl feels warm. Remove the bowl from the water and add half the oil drop by drop, whisking constantly. Continue adding the oil in a very thin stream, whisking vigorously. If the oil is not immediately absorbed, stop pouring and whisk. If the sauce separates, beat a teaspoon or two of hot water into it before adding more oil. Add vinegar, salt, and pepper to taste.

Variations:
For a heartier mayonnaise, use half olive oil and half vegetable or peanut oil. For herb mayonnaise, add 1 or 2 tablespoons of minced fresh herbs at the end.

Sauce Vinaigrette

Oil and Vinegar Dressing

Makes about ⅓ cup

The recipe for vinaigrette is very flexible, depending on what you prefer and what kind of salad you are preparing. As you can see, the basic proportion of ingredients I use is three or four parts oil to one part vinegar, according to the strength of the vinegar. You may replace part or all of the vinegar with lemon juice, or with lime juice, which I prefer because it is not so acid.

The oil should suit the salad. With strongly flavored or bitter greens I like to use part or all olive oil and some garlic in the dressing. For plain Boston lettuce I use peanut oil (which is almost tasteless) with lime juice, a little mustard, and some minced chives and chervil. Green beans are enhanced by a proportion of walnut oil, as are any salads garnished with walnuts. The possibilities are endless if you select your ingredients with imagination and sensitivity.

> **Salt and freshly ground pepper, to taste**
> **1 tablespoon red wine vinegar**
> **½ tablespoon lemon juice**
> **3 to 4 tablespoons salad oil**

Put the salt, pepper, vinegar, and lemon juice in a small bowl and mix well. Then add the oil slowly, mixing constantly, until the ingredients are blended.

Vinaigrette Moutardée

Robust Vinaigrette

Makes about ½ cup

Salt and freshly ground pepper, to taste
A little grated fresh garlic
1½ tablespoons red wine vinegar
2 tablespoons Dijon mustard
3 tablespoons vegetable oil
4 tablespoons olive oil

Mix all the ingredients except the oil thoroughly together in a small mixing bowl, then add the oil in a thin stream, stirring constantly, until the vinaigrette is blended.

Vinaigrette à l'Huile de Noix

Walnut Vinaigrette

Makes about ½ cup

4 tablespoons vegetable oil
2 tablespoons walnut oil
2 tablespoons lime juice
¼ teaspoon dry mustard
Salt and freshly ground pepper, to taste

Whisk the ingredients together in a bowl or shake them in a tightly closed jar.

BREADS AND PASTRIES

Biscuits à la Cuiller

Ladyfingers

Makes about 36

1 cup cake flour
4 egg yolks
¾ cup sugar
1 teaspoon vanilla extract
4 egg whites
Pinch of salt
Powdered sugar (for dusting)

Sift the flour onto a piece of wax paper. With an electric mixer or by hand, beat the egg yolks with all but 2 tablespoons of the sugar in a large bowl for several minutes, until they are thick and light in color. Add the vanilla and mix well.

In another bowl, beat the egg whites with a pinch of salt until they form soft peaks. Sprinkle with the remaining 2 tablespoons of sugar and continue beating until they form stiff peaks. Fold the egg whites gently into the yolk mixture, one-third at a time, alternating with the sifted flour. Don't worry if the mixture is not completely homogenous.

Using a pastry bag fitted with a large round tip, pipe the batter in 4-inch "fingers" onto a greased and floured baking sheet, spacing them at least 1 inch apart. Dust them lightly with powdered sugar and bake in a preheated 300°F oven until they are lightly browned, about 20 minutes. Remove the ladyfingers and cool them on wire racks.

Pâte Brisée

Short Pie Pastry

*Makes about ¾ pound, enough to line one
12-inch or two 7- or 8-inch tart shells*

6 tablespoons unsalted butter, cold
1½ cups all-purpose flour
2 large eggs
Pinch of salt

Cut the butter into tablespoons and put it in a food processor with the flour; mix until crumbly. In a bowl, beat the eggs with the salt (omit the salt if you use salted butter), and pour them into the flour mixture while the machine is running. As soon as the dough begins to form a ball, stop the processor and remove it. With floured hands, shape the dough into a thick patty; wrap it in wax paper and chill it for at least ½ hour before using it.

Alternative method: To mix the pastry by hand, sift the flour into a mixing bowl and cut in the butter with two knives or a pastry fork until the mixture is crumbly. Beat the eggs with the salt and add them to the flour mixture. Mix the dough lightly with your fingers or a pastry fork, pulling the dry portions into the moist ones. When the dough is fairly well mixed, place it on a floured work surface (preferably marble) and spread the dough by sliding the heel of your hand against the work surface to incorporate the butter completely. Work quickly in small areas, gathering the dough back into a ball with a pastry scraper. Be careful not to overwork the pastry or melt the butter. Shape the dough into a thick patty, wrap it in wax paper, and chill it for at least ½ hour.

Pâte Feuilletée

Puff Pastry

Makes about 1 pound

1 cup all-purpose flour, plus flour for dusting
¾ cup cake flour
2 tablespoons butter, cut in 4 pieces, plus 6 ounces
      (1½ sticks) cold unsalted butter
Pinch of salt
½ cup ice water, more if necessary

To make the *détrempe*, the dough into which you will fold the butter, put the all-purpose flour, ½ cup of cake flour, the 2 tablespoons of butter, and salt into a food processor. Blend until the butter is evenly distributed. With the machine running, pour ½ cup of ice water through the feed tube; if the dough doesn't begin to form a ball, add more ice water by tablespoonfuls until the dough can be massed together. However, it should not be sticky. Press it into a thick patty, dust it with flour, wrap, and chill it.

Using a rolling pin, roll or pound the cold butter between two pieces of wax paper, gradually adding the remaining ¼ cup of cake flour until it is all used. The butter will soften and become quite pliable and elastic. Do not let it start to melt; it should be about the same consistency as the *détrempe*. Form it into a 6-inch square.

Chill the work surface by placing several ice-cube trays on it before beginning the puff pastry and, later, while the dough is resting. Wipe it before using, and dust it with plenty of flour. Work quickly.

Remove the *détrempe* from the refrigerator and roll it out from the center in four opposing directions, as on a compass. It should be a rough square of about 12 to 14 inches from north to south and from east to west, and slightly thicker in the center. Place the butter diagonally across the center and fold the triangular sides of the dough around it, enclosing it like an envelope. Press the overlapping edges to seal it.

On a well-floured surface, roll out the pastry package, seam side down, to form a rectangle about three and a half times its original length. Fold it in thirds along its length to form a square again. Rotate the dough so the open side is on your right and the fold is on the left, like a book. Roll it out again to about three and a half times its length, and fold again in thirds. You have now given the dough two "turns." Wrap it and chill it for at least ½ hour to rest the dough.

Repeat the same procedure of rolling and folding four more times, resting the dough after every two turns. After six turns you may roll the pastry to whatever shape you wish, or keep it in the refrigerator for up to one week until you are ready to use it. The pastry may also be frozen for up to three months.

Pâte Demi-Feuilletée

Demi-Puff Pastry

Makes about 1 pound

10 tablespoons unsalted butter
1 cup minus 2 tablespoons all-purpose flour, plus
    flour for dusting
⅔ cup cake flour
½ teaspoon salt
½ cup ice water

Cut the butter into about 20 pieces and place it in the freezer for ½ hour, until it is very hard. Mix the flour and salt in a food processor (use less salt if you are using salted butter). Add the butter and pulse the mixture about six times, until the butter is in pieces the size of large peas. Add the ice water with the machine running; stop after 10 seconds. You should still be able to see pieces of butter, and the dough won't really form a ball.

Empty the work bowl onto a lightly floured, chilled work surface (preferably marble). Pat the dough into a rectangle about 1 inch thick and 12 to 14 inches long. It will look messy, but don't worry. Smooth the surface with a floured rolling pin. Using something large and flat for a scraper, such as the bottom of a tart mold or a small cookie sheet, fold the dough in thirds, bringing the two ends toward the middle and overlapping them completely in three layers (this is called a turn).

Slide the scraper under the dough and turn it ninety degrees, so the fold is on your left and the open side on your right, like a book. Reflour the work surface. As best you can, roll the dough into a rectangle about 12 inches long, using plenty of flour; press with your hands to neaten the sides. Fold the dough in thirds, as before, and rotate it so the open side is on your right. Repeat the procedure two more times, rolling the dough out to a rectangle about 14 inches long and folding it in thirds, by which time the dough will be smoother and more uniform but long streaks of butter will still be visible under the surface. Make four impressions with your fingertips on the top of the dough to indicate the four turns it has had. Wrap the dough in wax paper and chill it for at least ½ hour.

After it has chilled, give the dough two more turns, rolling it out to a rectangle and folding as before. You may keep the pastry for up to a week in the refrigerator, or you may freeze it. When you are ready to use it, form it as desired and chill before baking.

Pâte Sucrée

Sweet Pie Pastry

*Makes about ¾ pound, enough for one large or
two small tart shells*

1½ cups all-purpose flour
½ cup powdered sugar or ⅓ cup granulated sugar
6 tablespoons butter
2 egg yolks
Cold water as necessary
½ teaspoon vanilla extract

Put the flour and sugar in a food processor, add the butter, and
mix until crumbly. Beat the egg yolks in a bowl with a tablespoon
of cold water and the vanilla, then pour them into the flour mixture while the machine is running. If necessary, add more water by
tablespoonfuls until the dough begins to form a ball. Remove it,
shape it into a thick patty, wrap it in wax paper, and chill it for at
least ½ hour before using.

Brioche

Serves 6 to 8

1 package active dry yeast
1 tablespoon very warm water
2 tablespoons sugar
2 cups flour
½ teaspoon salt (if you use unsalted butter)
3 eggs
4 ounces (1 stick) butter, softened

Dissolve the yeast in the warm water and add the sugar. Allow the mixture to stand for 5 to 10 minutes, until bubbles appear on the surface, to proof the yeast. Sift the flour and salt into a large bowl, then add the yeast mixture and eggs. Stir the dough to mix the ingredients, then knead it with a slapping motion against the sides of the bowl or on a marble surface. (You may also use a mixer with a dough hook.) Incorporate the softened butter into the dough, continuing to knead until the dough is smooth and elastic. Cover it and let it rise in a buttered bowl until it has doubled in volume, about 2 hours. Punch it down and roll it into small balls. Place these in well-buttered muffin tins or small molds, half-filling each container with dough. Let the brioches rise until almost doubled, 1 to 1½ hours, then bake them in a preheated 425°F oven for 12 to 15 minutes. Cool before serving.

Pâte à Foncer

Quiche Dough

*Makes about ¾ pound, enough for one large or
two small quiches*

1½ cups all-purpose flour
6 tablespoons cold butter or shortening, cut into
    tablespoons
1 tablespoon oil
About 3 tablespoons ice water
Pinch of salt

Put the flour and butter or shortening in a food processor and mix
them until they are crumbly. In a bowl, beat the oil and water with
the salt, and pour them into the flour mixture while the machine is
running, adding more water by tablespoonfuls, if necessary, until
the dough begins to form a ball. Remove the dough and flatten it,
shaping it into a large patty about 1 inch thick. Wrap it in wax
paper and chill it for at least ½ hour before rolling it out.

FAVORITE
RECIPES

FIRST COURSES
AND LIGHT ENTRÉES

Oeufs Cressonière

Poached Eggs with Watercress

Serves 4

4 eggs
Salt
Vinegar
2 medium tomatoes
1 cup watercress, washed and with stems removed
1 cup cream
Freshly ground pepper
Nutmeg

Poach the eggs in simmering water to which you have added a pinch of salt and several tablespoons of vinegar. You may poach them ahead of time and keep them in cool water until you are ready to use them. Drop them briefly in simmering water to re-heat.

Cut the tomatoes in half horizontally and scoop out the insides. Salt them and drain them for several minutes. Purée the watercress in a blender or food processor. Transfer it to a medium-sized saucepan, add the cream and salt, pepper, and nutmeg to taste, and reduce the mixture by one-third over moderate heat.

Place the hot poached eggs in the tomato shells, top them with the hot sauce, and serve immediately.

Crème de Chou-Fleur

Cauliflower Soup

Serves 8

1 medium cauliflower (about 1½ pounds),
    trimmed
1 small potato, peeled
* 3½ to 4 cups chicken stock
* Bouquet garni with tarragon sprigs
¾ cup cream
Salt and freshly ground pepper
Nutmeg
Pinch of curry powder
Lemon juice
Minced chives and tarragon (for garnish)

In a large saucepan over moderate heat, cook the cauliflower and potato in 2½ cups of chicken stock with the bouquet garni, covered, until very tender. Purée the vegetables and stock in a blender or food processor and return them to the pan. Add the cream and as much additional stock as necessary to thin the soup to the desired consistency. Add the seasonings and lemon juice to taste. Serve the soup hot or cold, sprinkled with chives and tarragon.

Feuilletés aux Asperges

Asparagus in Puff Pastry

Serves 8

1 pound asparagus
* 1¼ pounds puff pastry
2 egg yolks
1 teaspoon water
Salt and freshly ground pepper

Trim and peel the asparagus. Steam or simmer it until just tender, then drain it and pat it dry. Cut it into ½-inch pieces, reserving the tips.

Divide the pastry in half. Roll one half into a rectangle ¼ inch thick and about 12 by 20 inches. Beat the egg yolks and water with a pinch of salt and brush the rectangle with them. Arrange the asparagus on top of the pastry in eight portions, distributing the tips equally. Sprinkle it with salt and pepper. Roll out the remaining pastry into a slightly larger rectangle and place it on top, pressing to seal the two pastry rectangles between the mounds of asparagus. Cut the pastry into individual servings, place them on a baking sheet, and chill them for at least ½ hour in the freezer.

Bake the pastry cases in a preheated 375°F oven until they are golden brown, about ½ hour. Serve them hot, with hollandaise sauce (p. 249) in a sauceboat.

Coeurs d'Artichauts
à la Mousse de Saumon

Artichoke Bottoms
with Salmon Mousse

Serves 6

6 large artichokes
Lemon juice
1 cup vinegar
1 pound fresh salmon, boned
2 ounces smoked salmon
1 egg
* 1½ to 2 cups *crème fraîche* or heavy cream
Freshly ground pepper
Salt (optional)

Trim the raw artichokes to remove the leaves and shape them (as described on p. 29), rubbing the cut surface immediately with lemon juice; or cook them whole and pull off all the leaves, trim off the stem, and scoop out the choke afterward. Cook the raw artichoke bottoms in salted water with the vinegar for about 15 or 20 minutes; whole artichokes will take 35 to 45 minutes.

Purée the fresh salmon in a food processor. It is not necessary to remove the skin first; after about ½ minute it will separate from the fish and you can stop the machine and remove it from the work bowl. Add the smoked salmon and run the machine about 1 minute more, until the fish is a very smooth purée. Add the egg, incorporate it well, and add the *crème fraîche* or cream by large spoonfuls. It is not necessary to chill the fish mixture before adding the cream unless it has become warm, in which case you should place the entire work bowl in the freezer.

After adding about 1½ cups of cream, poach a small amount of the salmon mixture in simmering salted water to check the consistency and the seasoning. You may not need salt, because the smoked fish provides enough. Season, and if the mixture is too dense, add more cream.

Place the cooked artichoke bottoms in a buttered baking dish. Using a pastry bag or spoon, fill them with salmon mousse. Cover and heat the dish for 15 minutes in a preheated 325°F oven. (This dish may be made several hours ahead of time and baked just before serving.) Serve the artichokes with a sauce such as hollandaise (p. 249) or *beurre blanc* (p. 248).

Homard à la Normande

Lobster with Calvados and Cream

Multiply these ingredients by the number of people you will be serving.

> 1 lobster tail
> About 1 tablespoon butter
> 2 tablespoons Calvados
> 3 tablespoons cream
> Salt
> Cayenne

Remove the lobster meat from the shell, keeping the shell intact. Chop the meat coarsely and sauté it in a skillet over fairly high heat in a little butter. Remove it when just cooked and deglaze the pan with the Calvados. Add the cream and reduce it by half, then return the meat to the pan, season the sauce to taste, and spoon the mixture into the reserved shell. Serve the lobster hot.

Brioche au Crabe

Brioche Filled with Crab

Serves 6

For the brioche:
1 package active dry yeast
2 tablespoons very warm water
2 tablespoons sugar
2 cups flour
½ teaspoon salt (if you use unsalted butter)
3 eggs
4 ounces (1 stick) cold butter

For the filling
8 ounces fresh mushrooms, sliced
3 tablespoons butter
Juice of ½ lemon
Salt and freshly ground pepper
8 ounces crabmeat, cleaned
* Fish stock or clam juice (optional)
3 tablespoons cornstarch
½ cup cream

To make the brioche:
Dissolve the yeast in the warm water with the sugar. Allow it to stand for 5 to 10 minutes, until bubbles appear on the surface, to proof the yeast. In a large food processor with the plastic blade in place, or in an electric mixer with a dough hook, combine the flour and salt, add the eggs and yeast mixture, and mix well. Cut the cold butter into tablespoons and gradually add them to the dough, kneading for several minutes until the butter has been completely incorporated. Stop the machine occasionally to touch the dough; it should not be warmer than body temperature. Knead for as long

as possible without letting the dough become too warm — which will happen more quickly in a food processor. (If you use a small food processor, add the butter to the flour at the beginning. Process it until crumbly and proceed as above for moist ingredients.)

Place the dough in a buttered bowl, cover it, and let it rise in a warm, draft-free spot until doubled in volume, about 2 hours. Punch it down. Cut the dough into 8 or 10 pieces and roll the pieces into balls. Place these in a heavily buttered 6-cup ring mold, almost touching, and allow them to rise again until nearly doubled, about 1 to 1½ hours.

Bake the brioche in a preheated 375°F oven for 18 to 20 minutes or until done. Let it stand for about 5 minutes in the pan before you unmold it onto a serving platter. You may make the brioche ahead, cool it, and reheat it in foil before serving.

To make the filling:
Cook the mushrooms in a large skillet or saucepan in 1 tablespoon of butter, the lemon juice, a little water, and salt and pepper to taste. The mushrooms should be almost covered with liquid. Simmer them for 10 to 15 minutes, then drain them, reserving the cooking liquid. Drain the crabmeat and add its juice to the mushroom cooking liquid. Boil the liquid to reduce it to 1 cup, or add stock or clam juice to make 1 cup.

Melt the remaining 2 tablespoons of butter in a saucepan. Add the cornstarch and cook until it just begins to color. Remove it from the heat and add the mushroom-and-crab liquid, stirring constantly. Bring this sauce to a boil, whisking, then add the cream, crabmeat, and mushrooms. Taste the mixture and correct the seasoning.

To serve:
Place the warm brioche in the center of a serving platter. Fill the center with the hot crab-and-mushroom filling and serve immediately.

ENTRÉES

Filets de Sole Cipriani

Fillets of Sole with Two Sauces

Serves 6

This recipe reminds me of a wonderful week I spent at the Hotel Cipriani in Venice, demonstrating French cooking in a room overlooking the lagoon. This recipe was given to me by the manager of the hotel, Mr. Ruscoli.

6 small fillets of sole, bones and heads removed

For the fish stock:
1 tablespoon butter
1 onion, sliced
Bones and head from the sole
2 cups white wine
2 cups water
1 carrot, sliced
1 stalk celery, sliced
5 peppercorns
1 small bay leaf

For the hollandaise:
2 egg yolks
1 tablespoon water
Salt

2 tablespoons lemon juice
4 ounces (1 stick) butter, melted and cooled

For the velouté:
1 cup fish stock
1 tablespoon butter
1 tablespoon flour
¼ cup heavy cream

Salt and freshly ground pepper
½ cup freshly grated Parmesan cheese

To make the fish stock:
Melt 1 tablespoon of butter in a large saucepan, add the onion, and cook until transparent. Add the fish bones and head, wine, water, sliced carrot and celery, peppercorns, and bay leaf. Bring the mixture to a boil and then simmer it gently for 20 minutes. Strain the stock.

To make the hollandaise:
In a heavy saucepan, combine the egg yolks, water, and a pinch of salt. Beat until the eggs are foamy. Place the pan over very low heat and beat until the eggs are thick and creamy yellow. Beat in the lemon juice. Slowly add the butter in a thin trickle, beating all the time. As the sauce begins to thicken, add the butter a little faster, until it has all been added. Keep the sauce warm over hot water.

To make the velouté:
Bring 1 cup of fish stock to a boil; remove it from the heat. Melt the butter in another saucepan and add the flour. Cook for several minutes, but do not brown. Add the hot fish stock all at once, beating well, then cook the sauce over low heat until it thickens, about 10 minutes. Remove it from the heat and beat in the cream. Keep it warm.

To prepare the dish:
Place the remaining fish stock in a heavy skillet. Bring it to a boil, then reduce it to a simmer. Poach the sole fillets in the stock until

they are just opaque, about 2 or 3 minutes. Remove and drain the fillets; keep them warm.

Butter a flat, ovenproof baking dish. Arrange the fish fillets in it in a slightly overlapping pattern. Mix the two sauces together, season them to taste with salt and pepper, and thin them with a little more fish stock if necessary. Spread the mixed sauce over the fish. Sprinkle Parmesan cheese over the top and place the dish in a preheated 450°F oven until the sauce is brown and bubbling, about 10 to 15 minutes. Serve at once.

Matelote de Poisson au Vin Blanc

Fish Stew with White Wine

Serves 6

2 pounds of any available white freshwater fish
    (carp, perch, trout, etc.), boned and
    skinned and with heads and tails removed
Salt and freshly ground pepper
¼ pound salt pork, cut into ¼-inch cubes,
    blanched, and rinsed
1 or 2 cloves garlic, crushed
2 medium onions, sliced
½ pound small mushrooms, washed and with
    stems removed
½ cup dry white wine
* Bouquet garni
3 tablespoons chopped parsley
2 tablespoons Cognac
12 slices country bread
½ cup oil
2 tablespoons flour
4 tablespoons butter, softened

Cut the fish into 2-inch chunks. Season it to taste with salt and pepper. Render the salt pork in a skillet until it is brown and crisp; remove it from the skillet and reserve it. Add the fish, garlic, onions, mushrooms, wine, bouquet garni, and 2 tablespoons of parsley to the skillet containing the pork drippings. Bring the mixture to a boil. Warm the Cognac, add it to the stew, ignite it, and allow the flames to die. Simmer the mixture for 15 to 20 minutes, or until the fish is done. Remove the fish.

Make the croutons by cutting 2-inch rounds of bread about ⅜ inch thick and frying them in a skillet in ½ inch of very hot oil until they are golden brown. To serve six people you will need twelve croutons. Drain them on paper towels.

To make a *beurre manié*, mash the flour and softened butter with a fork until mixed. Slowly add this to the stew, stirring constantly. Simmer until the sauce is thick and smooth, about 5 minutes. Add water if necessary. Return the fish to the sauce.

To serve, arrange the croutons around the edge of a shallow serving dish. Spoon in the fish stew and serve it hot, sprinkled with the remaining chopped parsley.

Délice de Saumon, Coulis de Tomates Fraîches

Cold Salmon Mousse with Fresh Tomato Sauce

Serves 6 to 8

For the mousse:
1 quart water
1 cup dry white wine
1 carrot, sliced
1 onion, sliced
* Bouquet garni
12 peppercorns
½ pound fresh salmon
2 tablespoons butter plus 2 ounces (½ stick)
    softened butter
2 tablespoons flour
1 cup milk
2 slices raw onion
1 small bay leaf
Nutmeg
2 to 3 tablespoons cream or sour cream
2 tablespoons sherry, or to taste

For the sauce:
2 pounds fresh ripe tomatoes
1 tablespoon minced fresh dill
1 tablespoon minced chives
1 tablespoon minced chervil or parsley
Pinch of curry powder
Salt and freshly ground pepper

For the garnish:
1 cucumber, thinly sliced

1 lemon, thinly sliced
Smoked salmon (optional)
Fresh dill

To make the mousse:
Make a court bouillon (p. 241) with the water, wine, carrot, onion, bouquet garni, and 6 peppercorns; simmer it, uncovered, for 20 minutes. Poach the salmon gently until it is cooked, about 20 minutes. Cool the fish in the court bouillon, then remove it and discard the skin and bones.

Melt the 2 tablespoons of butter in a heavy saucepan; add the flour and cook gently for 2 or 3 minutes, without browning. In a separate saucepan, bring the milk to a boil with the onion slices, 6 peppercorns, the bay leaf, and nutmeg to taste; remove it from the heat and set it aside for a few minutes for the flavorings to infuse the milk. Add the milk mixture to the flour and butter, bring it to a boil, and cook, stirring constantly, until it thickens, 3 to 5 minutes. Let it cool to room temperature.

In a food processor or blender, purée the salmon, adding the cooled white sauce gradually. Then add the softened butter, cream or sour cream, and sherry. Mix well; taste the mousseline and correct the seasoning. As it is served cold, it should be fairly highly seasoned.

Turn the mousse into a well-oiled mold and chill it for at least ½ hour.

To make the sauce:
Quarter the tomatoes and purée them in a blender or food processor. Strain the purée to remove peels, seeds, and stems, then season it with the fresh herbs, curry powder, and salt and pepper to taste.

To serve:
Unmold the mousse onto a serving platter and garnish it with thin slices of cucumber and lemon. Add strips of smoked salmon, if you wish, and sprigs of fresh dill. Serve it with the fresh tomato sauce.

Poulet Cauchois

Norman-Style Chicken

Serves 6

We live in a part of Normandy that is called the Pays de Caux, the "chalk country." Chalk is present everywhere, especially on the cliffs by the seashore, which are known all over the world because they were painted in Étretat by the Impressionists.

Naturally, the inhabitants of this region are known as Cauchois and Cauchoises. *Poulet Cauchois* is a local specialty, which is why I have included it among my favorites. It is also delicious!

> 1 cup plus 2 tablespoons butter
> 1 pound fresh white bread crumbs
> ¼ pound bacon
> 3 pounds Golden Delicious or Granny Smith apples
> Pinch of sage
> Pinch of thyme
> A 4-pound chicken
> Salt and freshly ground pepper
> 2 tablespoons port
> 1 cup heavy cream
> 1 jar red currant jelly, warmed

In a heat-resistant baking dish, melt the cup of butter. Add the bread crumbs and sauté them until golden over high heat. Stir them often. When they are done, remove them and set them aside to drain on a paper towel. Cut the bacon into small chunks, blanch it in boiling water for 5 minutes, and sauté it lightly in the remaining butter. Drain the bacon pieces on a paper towel.

Peel 3 apples, core them, and cut them into eight pieces. Sauté them in the bacon-fat-and-butter mixture. When the apples are soft but not falling apart, add the sage and thyme. Add the bread crumbs and mix well.

Stuff the chicken with the bread-crumb-and-apple mixture, then truss it. Butter a sheet of parchment. Place the chicken in a large casserole with a lid, season it with salt and pepper to taste, and cover it with the parchment. Cook it, covered, in a preheated 400°F oven for 1 hour.

Peel, core, and halve the remaining apples. Cook them with 2 tablespoons of butter in a skillet over low heat for 10 minutes.

When the chicken is tender, remove it from the oven and keep it hot. Lift off the parchment. Remove the apples from the heat. Deglaze the casserole with the port, then add the cream and boil the sauce for 8 to 10 minutes. Check the seasoning and correct it if necessary.

Arrange the chicken on a large serving platter. Divide the apples around it and spoon some of the red currant jelly over them. Pour some of the sauce over the meat and serve the chicken very hot, with the remaining sauce in a sauceboat.

Fricassée de Poulet au Vinaigre de Framboise

Sautéed Chicken with Raspberry Vinegar

Serves 4

    A 4-pound chicken
    ⅔ cup butter
    Salt and freshly ground pepper
    3 tablespoons raspberry vinegar
  * 1 cup brown stock
    ½ cup heavy cream
    1 pound fresh raspberries (for garnish)

Cut the chicken into eight pieces. Wash the giblets and reserve them.

In a frying pan, melt ½ cup of butter; add the chicken, season it to taste with salt and pepper, and cook for 20 minutes, turning the pieces to brown them evenly. When the chicken is cooked, remove it from the pan and keep it warm in a preheated 350°F oven.

Add the remaining butter and the giblets to the pan and deglaze it with the raspberry vinegar. Let this sauce reduce almost totally on the stove, then add the stock and cream. Bring it to a boil and cook for 8 to 10 minutes, until the sauce is slightly thick. Taste it and correct the seasoning if necessary.

Remove the chicken from the oven and place the pieces on a serving platter. Strain the raspberry sauce over them and garnish the dish with the fresh raspberries.

Pigeons aux Gousses d'Ail en Chemise

Roast Pigeons with Garlic

¾ cup butter
½ teaspoon thyme
6 pigeons, cleaned, with livers
Salt and freshly ground pepper
28 large cloves garlic, separated but not peeled
2 tablespoons Cognac
* ¾ cup chicken stock

Put 1 tablespoon of butter and a pinch of thyme in the cavity of each bird and truss the pigeons with string. Season them with salt and pepper. Melt the rest of the butter in a heavy ovenproof skillet and brown the birds on all sides. Arrange the garlic around the birds and put the pan in a preheated 400°F oven to roast for 20 minutes. Baste the pigeons frequently with the pan juices.

When the birds are cooked, remove them and the garlic from the pan and set aside 10 of the garlic cloves for the sauce. In the same pan, brown the reserved livers. Pour in the Cognac and heat well. Purée the livers, 10 cloves of garlic, and pan juices in a food processor or blender, and strain it or pass it through a food mill.

Bring the stock to a boil in a large frying pan. Add the liver-and-garlic purée and whisk the sauce until it is smooth. Add the birds and heat them through.

To serve, remove the trussing strings and arrange the pigeons on a platter with the remaining garlic. Nap them with the sauce and serve immediately.

Variation:
Small Cornish game hens may be substituted for the pigeons.

VEGETABLES AND SALADS

Oignons Nouveaux au Beurre

Steamed Scallions

Serves 6

36 large scallions of a uniform size
3 tablespoons butter
Salt and freshly ground pepper
* *Sauce vinaigrette*
3 or 4 hard-boiled egg yolks, sieved

Wash and trim the scallions, leaving about 2 inches of green. Steam them in a saucepan until they are almost tender, and drain them on paper towels.

Just before serving, melt the butter in a large skillet and toss the scallions to reheat them and coat them with butter, shaking the pan to avoid burning. Season them to taste with salt and pepper. Arrange the cooled scallions on a platter and sprinkle them with *Sauce vinaigrette* and sieved hard-boiled egg yolks. Serve them cold but not chilled.

Riz Créole

Baked Rice

Serves 8

4 ounces (1 stick) butter
1 pound long-grain rice
1 quart water
1 teaspoon salt
* **Bouquet garni (optional)**

Melt the butter in a heavy ovenproof skillet or cast-iron casserole with a lid. Add the rice and cook it until it is opaque. Add the water, salt, and a bouquet garni if you wish; cover the rice with buttered parchment and the lid. Bake it in a preheated 375°F oven for 18 minutes without stirring, then check to see if the rice is tender. If all the water has been absorbed and the rice is still hard, add ½ cup more water and cook for 10 minutes more. If the rice has not absorbed the water and is almost tender, uncover it, leaving the paper in place, and bake it 5 to 10 minutes more.

Salade de Concombres et de Capucines

Cucumber and Nasturtium Salad

Serves 4 to 6

2 cucumbers
36 small nasturtium leaves
1 teaspoon Dijon mustard
2 tablespoons red wine vinegar
6 tablespoons olive oil
Salt and freshly ground pepper
2 tablespoons finely chopped fresh tarragon
6 nasturtium flowers (optional)

Peel and slice the cucumbers in thin rounds. Wash the nasturtium leaves, remove their stems, and drain.

Combine the mustard and vinegar in a bowl and stir until well blended. Add the olive oil and salt and pepper to taste, and blend well. Stir in the tarragon.

When you are ready to serve, combine the cucumbers and nasturtium leaves in a salad bowl; add the vinaigrette dressing and toss well. Garnish the salad with nasturtium flowers if you wish.

DESSERTS

Entremets de Figues à la Crème

Layered Dessert of Figs and Cream

Serves 8

The figs must marinate for several days before you assemble this dish.

> 5 pounds fresh figs
> 1 cup dry sherry
> 1 cup Cognac
> ½ cup crème de cacao
> ½ to 1 cup sugar
> 2 cups heavy cream
> 2½ cups coarsely chopped walnuts

Peel the figs and halve them, or quarter them if they are large. Marinate them in the sherry, Cognac, crème de cacao, and sugar to taste for two to four days, covered, in the refrigerator.

The day you are serving the dessert, whip the cream. Arrange a layer of figs in the bottom of a glass salad bowl, sprinkle them with chopped walnuts, cover with whipped cream, and repeat in this order to make about six layers, finishing with whipped cream. Chill the dessert covered for 6 hours in the refrigerator before serving.

Terrine de Fruits

Fresh Fruit Terrine

Serves 10

2 envelopes gelatin
Juice of 1 lemon
¼ cup cold water
1½ cups orange juice
⅓ cup confectioner's sugar
Grated zest of 1 orange and 1 lemon
½ teaspoon almond extract
¼ cup Cointreau or Grand Marnier
1 cup whipped cream
1 pint strawberries, washed, dried, and hulled
1 large or 2 small oranges, peeled and cut into
     sections without the membrane

For the coulis:
2 pints strawberries or 1 large bag frozen berries
Juice of 1 lemon
½ cup confectioner's sugar, or to taste

In a small saucepan or heatproof dish, soften the gelatin in the juice of 1 lemon mixed with ¼ cup cold water. Heat the mixture to dissolve the gelatin, stirring until no crystals remain. In a large bowl, combine the orange juice and confectioner's sugar and add the dissolved gelatin mixture. Add the grated zests of the orange and lemon, the almond extract, and the orange liqueur. Chill the mixture until it is quite thick and just on the verge of setting, then fold in the whipped cream.

    Dry the strawberries and oranges as much as possible and halve or quarter them lengthwise, depending on size. Put a layer of the gelatin mixture in the bottom of a large loaf pan; add a layer of strawberries and oranges, and alternate layers of gelatin and fruit until the pan is filled. Chill it for at least ½ hour, until the gelatin is firm.

To make the *coulis*, put the fresh or frozen strawberries in a food processor or blender with the juice of 1 lemon and ½ cup confectioner's sugar. Process or blend the mixture, adding more sugar if necessary. Strain the *coulis* to remove the seeds, then chill it.

To serve, unmold the terrine and surround it with some of the *coulis*. Serve the remaining *coulis* in a sauceboat.

Gâteau au Chocolat de Nancy

Chocolate Almond Cake

Serves 6

This recipe is from the east of France. The city of Nancy is in the province of Lorraine, which is close to the German border. One of my husband's ancestors was the last governor of Alsace-Lorraine, in 1787, before the French Revolution.

> 4 ounces (1 stick) butter
> ½ cup plus 2 tablespoons sugar
> 4 ounces semisweet chocolate, broken in pieces
> 4 egg yolks
> 1 tablespoon flour
> ⅓ cup ground almonds
> 1 teaspoon vanilla extract
> 4 egg whites
> Pinch of salt
> Powdered sugar (optional)

Cream the butter and ½ cup of sugar in a small bowl until they are light and fluffy. In a large bowl, gently melt the chocolate over warm (not hot) water, stirring until it is smooth. Add it to the butter mixture, beating constantly. The chocolate should not be hot enough to melt the butter. Add the egg yolks one at a time, beating continually, then add the flour, almonds, and vanilla.

In a separate bowl, beat the egg whites with a pinch of salt until they form soft peaks. Add the remaining 2 tablespoons of sugar and continue beating to form stiff peaks. Fold the egg whites delicately into the batter.

Line the bottom of a well-buttered and floured 9-inch cake pan with buttered and floured wax paper or parchment. Fill the pan with batter and bake it in a preheated 325°F oven until a knife inserted in the middle comes out clean, about 25 or 30 minutes.

Cool the cake in the pan for 5 minutes, then invert it onto a serving plate and remove the paper. Sprinkle it with powdered sugar if you wish.

Index